1978

PEOPLES OF THE EARTH

volume five
Islands
of the
Atlantic
including the
Caribbean

THE DANBURY PRESS

(Preceding page) More than a
thousand years ago the Viking
seafarers settled on the
Faroe Islands. They sailed
in their dragon-headed
longships past these same
skerries; they fished and
caught whales in the same
waters; they took birds and
birds' eggs from the same
cliffside nests.

Editorial Director **Tom Stacey**

Picture Director **Alexander Low**
Executive Editors **Katherine Ivens**
Robert Targett
Art Director **Tom Deas**
Assistant Editor **Elisabeth Meakin**
Project Co-ordinator **Anne Harrison**

Picture Research **Cheryl Moyer**
Fanya Aspler
Elly Beintema
Philippa Galloway
Claire Waterson
Editorial Assistants **Richard Carlisle**
Rosamund Ellis
Susan Rutherford
Xan Smiley
Design Assistants **Susan Forster**
Richard Kelly
Cartography **Ron Hayward**
Illustrations **Sandra Archibald**
Ron McTrusty

Production **Roger Multon**

The publishers gratefully acknowledge help from
the following organizations:
Royal Anthropological Institute, London
Musée de l'Homme, Paris
International African Institute, London
British Museum, London
Royal Geographical Society, London
Scott Polar Research Institute, Cambridge
Royal Asiatic Society, London
Royal Central Asian Society, London
Pitt-Rivers Museum, Oxford
Horniman Museum, London
Institute of Latin American Studies, London

PHOTOGRAPHIC CREDITS
Cover—**Jeffrey Foxx** (Woodfin Camp Associates), **Stephanie Dinkins,**
Homer Sykes (The John Hillelson Agency), **Jim McLagan** (Sunday
Times). 2,3—**Adam Woolfitt** (Susan Griggs). 16,17—**Marc Riboud**
(Magnum from the John Hillelson Agency). 18,19—**Fred Mayer**
(Woodfin Camp Associates). 20,21—**Marc Riboud** (Magnum from the
John Hillelson Agency) exc.bot.rt.—**Henri Cartier Bresson** (Magnum
from the John Hillelson Agency). 22,23—**Nicholas Sapieha** (Rapho
New York) exc.bot,rt.—**Fred Mayer** (Woodfin Camp Associates).
24 through 27—**Henri Cartier Bresson** and **Marc Riboud** (both Magnum
from the John Hillelson Agency). 28 through 32—**Ian Berry** (Magnum
from the John Hillelson Agency). 33—**John Launois** (Black Star New
York). 34,35—**S. Joses** (Woodfin Camp Associates). 36 through 45—
Jeffrey Foxx (Woodfin Camp Associates) exc top lt. 38 and bot.rt. 40—
S. Joses (Woodfin Camp Associates). 46 through 48—**Jonathan**
Trapman exc. top. rt. 48—**Jeffrey Foxx** (Woodfin Camp Associates).
50 through 52—**Charles Moore** (Black Star New York). 54—**Alexander**
Low. 55—**Bob Henriques** (Magnum from the John Hillelson Agency).
56,57—**Jeffrey Foxx** (Woodfin Camp Associates). 58,59—**Charles**
Harbutt (Magnum from the John Hillelson Agency), **Jeffrey Foxx** and
S. Joses (both Woodfin Camp Associates). 60,61—**Guido Mangold**
(Camera Press). 62,63—**Marilyn Silverstone** and **Charles Harbutt** (both
Magnum from the John Hillelson Agency). 64 through 67—Daily
Telegraph. 68—**Jeffrey Foxx** (Woodfin Camp Associates). 70—**Jean**
Loup-Fenouillet (Fotogram), **Mike Andrews, Fred Ward** (Black Star
New York). 72 through 79—**John de Visser.** 80—**Fred Bruemmer.** 82
through 91—**Adam Woolfitt** (Susan Griggs). 92 through 99—**Homer**
Sykes (The John Hillelson Agency). 100 through 111—**Stephanie**
Dinkins. 112 through 119—**Jim McLagan** (Argus South African
Newspapers) exc.bot.rt. 114—U.P.I. 120 through 125—**Tony Morrison,**
Marian Morrison (Keystone Press). 126,127—Daily Telegraph. 128—
Anthony Howarth, John Marmaras (Daily Telegraph). 129—**Alexander**
Low. 130 through 135—National Trust from Scotland exc.bot.rt. 132—
Charles Mclean, and bot.lt. and rt. 135—**Mario Ford.**

The DANBURY PRESS
a division of GROLIER ENTERPRISES INC.
Publisher
ROBERT B. CLARKE

© 1973 Europa Verlag

Library of Congress Catalog Card No. 72 85614

Printed in Italy by
Arnoldo Mondadori Editore, Verona

Contents

Supervisory Editor of the Series:
Professor Sir Edward Evans-Pritchard,
Fellow of All Souls, Professor of Social Anthropology,
University of Oxford, 1946-1970,
Chevalier de la Légion d'Honneur

Volume Editor:
Professor Fernando Henriques,
Center for Multi-Racial Studies,
University of Sussex, author of
Family and Colour in Jamaica etc

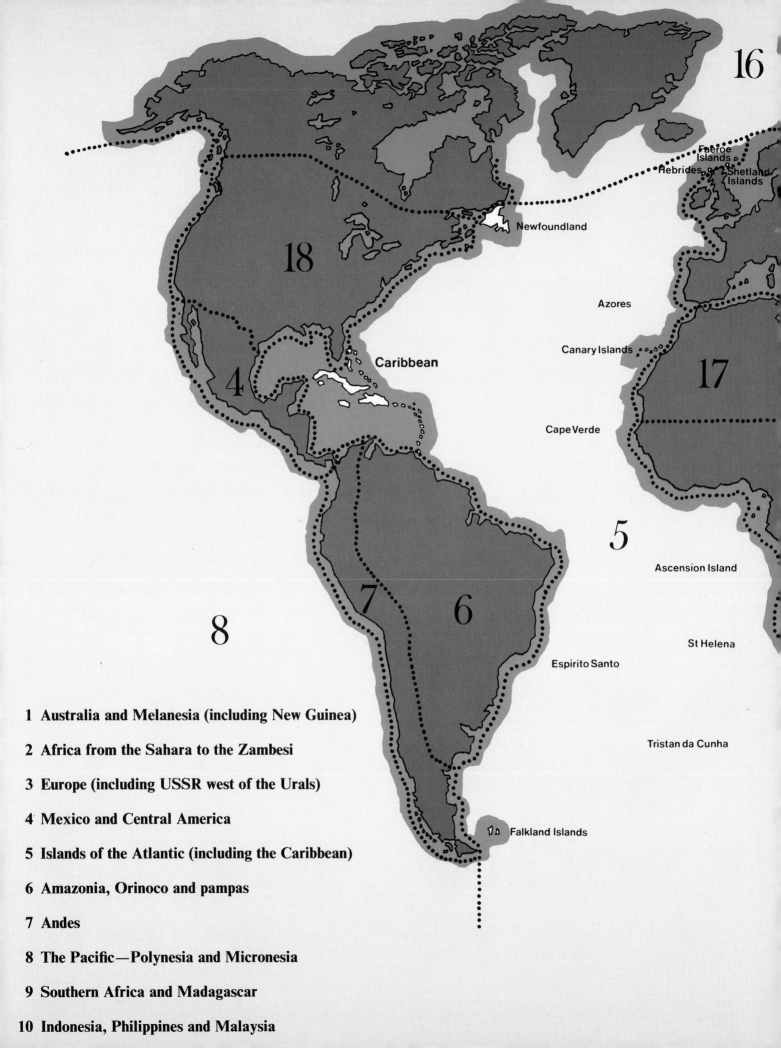

16

Faeroe Islands

Hebrides

Shetland Islands

Newfoundland

18

Azores

Caribbean

Canary Islands

17

Cape Verde

5

Ascension Island

4

7

6

St Helena

8

Espirito Santo

Tristan da Cunha

Falkland Islands

1 **Australia and Melanesia (including New Guinea)**

2 **Africa from the Sahara to the Zambesi**

3 **Europe (including USSR west of the Urals)**

4 **Mexico and Central America**

5 **Islands of the Atlantic (including the Caribbean)**

6 **Amazonia, Orinoco and pampas**

7 **Andes**

8 **The Pacific—Polynesia and Micronesia**

9 **Southern Africa and Madagascar**

10 **Indonesia, Philippines and Malaysia**

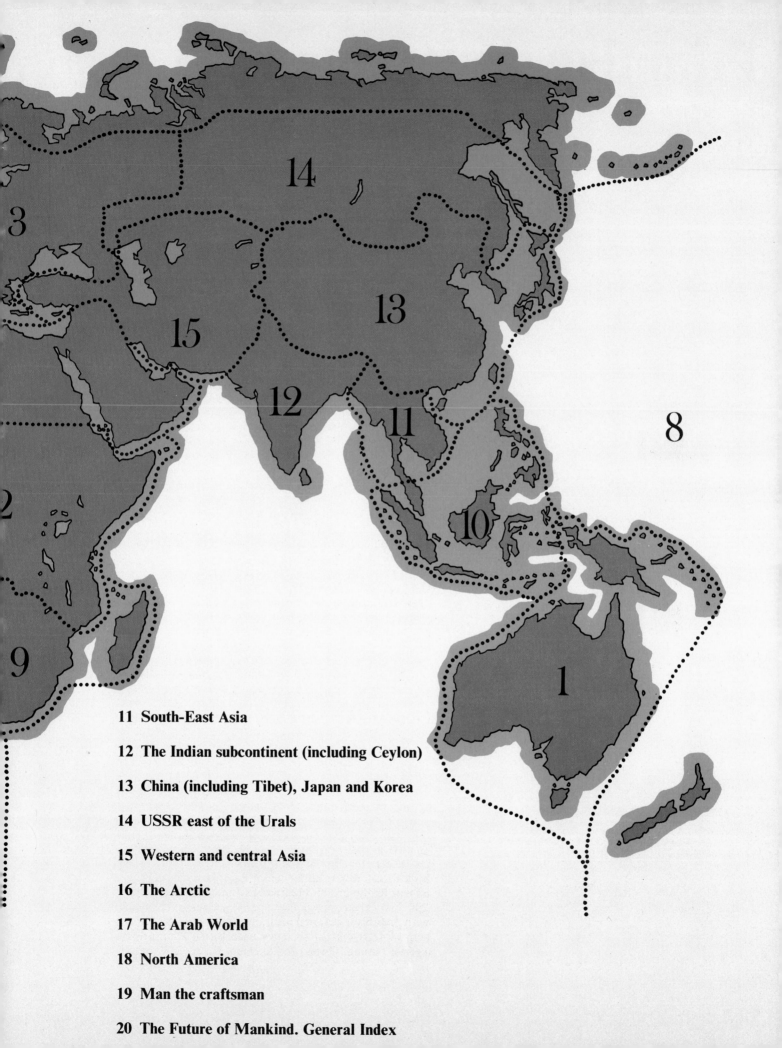

Primitive government

The simplest political system seems to be where one man, by his personal influence, comes to be the leading authority of a small band of hunters, fishers or collectors of wild produce. This type of leadership is also found among some cultivators: it is particularly common in relatively small Melanesian societies, which live by cultivating crops – especially the sweet potato – and by raising pigs.

Many tribes of hunters and fishermen have been studied by anthropologists. When anthropologists first knew the Bushmen of South Africa they were confined to the drier western regions of South Africa, Namibia, south-west Africa and Angola. Previously they had been widespread throughout southern Africa, where they left many of their beautiful rock-paintings, until they were driven from the richer parts of the land and were killed by the Nguni group of the Bantu-speaking peoples. The Bushmen roam the barren country, the men hunting and the women collecting roots and plants. Each band of ten to twenty men, mostly related to one another by descent or by families, claim a definite territory; although the boundaries are not clearly determined over a large area – in 1942 a British District Commissioner had to try to settle a dispute over hunting territory between bands in the Mashi River region whose central bases were 100 miles apart. According to Bushmen ideology – which is shared by other hunters such as the Australian Aborigines – ancestral connections with the land prevent one band from conquering the territory of another.

However, there are battles over territories and these have all to be defended against the encroachments of pastoral Hottentots and Bantu-speakers, with their hunting parties, cattle, and gardens. Authority in the bands of Bushmen, who are usually related, is exercised by the senior male of the line if he has suitable qualities. According to the Bushman code, if one man is aggrieved by the enchroachments of another he can in theory defend himself, possibly injuring or killing the offender; and again if one man is killed his nearest relatives can kill the offender. This killing – the unlimited vendetta – can go on interminably, as in Corsica and among the mountain people in and around American Kentucky – graphically described by Mark Twain in the story of *Huckleberry Finn*.

But hunting is a chancy business; clearly a hunting people cannot survive if there is continual quarrelling and killing. Men go out alone or in small parties in different directions in search of game. Some may find it, others may not. And it is characteristic of hunters and fishers that the man who gets game one day shares his kill with the band, for he knows that on another day he will be the grateful recipient of meat from another's kill. Just as our society uses specialized insurance firms, with possibly a national insurance scheme, as well as the help of relatives, all societies need forms of insurance against famine, illness, and accident. In societies which

Max Gluckman

have simpler, less differentiated institutions, insurance takes the form of mutual hospitality and gift-exchange – through links of family and marriage, or through friendship, trading partners or blood-brothers. Life in a hunting band compels this sharing. Internal quarrels have to be quickly settled.

The Bushmen settle their disputes by what has been called the 'talking match'. The offended state their grievances and the offenders their defense before the whole band, who listen and give judgement. The Bushmen's 'talking matches' are accompanied by a constant stream of gossip and scandal circulating among all members of the group. Anthropologists have recently focussed on the way gossip sets a level of conformity in every group: gossip and scandal can restrain people from breaking rules, influence the selection of suitable leaders and help a society to maintain its code or rules. Gossip and scandal can of course also be used by an individual for his own purpose. He can use it to crush a rival or enemy, or to gain information for profit.

The 'talking match' is a similar institution to the 'song contest' of the Arctic and Greenland Eskimo. The Eskimos, like other hunters, also have to search for their food in many directions on land, ice and sea. To amuse themselves in the long Arctic winter nights, men challenge each other to a contest of witty taunting songs, followed by a great feast. These contests are combined with an exchange of goods, between neighboring hunting bands – especially when one brings goods from the sea-coast and the other from inland. On these occasions each partner has to outdo the other in generosity, while simultaneously downing him with wit. And when a man feels he has been offended he challenges the offender to a contest and introduces into it a tale of extravagant – possibly absurd – allegations representing the details of his opponent's offense. According to the rules of the game, the contestant who shows that he has been affected by his opponent's allegations or insults, or by his physical pranks, is the loser. In all this the audience plays an important part. They applaud the complainant's gibes if they are convinced that he is in the right, and the wrongdoer who loses the contest is shown to have erred. The feast that follows is intended to cement a friendship between the two men at loggerheads.

Unless they were curbed, these Eskimos went in for unlimited vendettas. They evidently killed one another at a high rate. There are dramatic first-hand accounts of killings over women, trivial insults and teasing. And although there were Eskimo bands that believed that some female children should be killed, the resulting preponderance of males among children and young adults rapidly shifted to a preponderance of females as the hazards of life in the snowy wastes took toll of the men. If the Eskimos were to survive they too had to have some means beyond the 'song contest' of dealing with quarrels. In each band one man was endowed with authority based on his personal skills. He would consult the band informally about a recidivist wrongdoer and then having ensured the kin's agreement to avoid a vendetta he would either execute the wrongdoer himself or get a kinsman or kinswoman of the convicted man to take on the job.

The same system operated among some Kenyan people: a man the elders considered a persistent offender against tribal rules and peace could be eliminated, but only if his kin agreed and joined the execution party. Then when somebody fell ill a shaman would show by his divination that the patient had offended against the great spirits that watched over the world. The shaman would demand confession and amendment of behavior. Persistent offenses against the spirits could lead to a verdict of expulsion.

When the sea-coast Eskimo and the inland Eskimo hunt, when they try to outdo each other in generosity, and trade products of the sea and land with each other to their mutual advantage, the aim of the exchange is not so much for maximum gain – which they in fact regard as shameful – as for prestige. And it is upon a high regard for personal prestige that the continuation of law and maintenance of mutual obligations rests between many individuals and groups in many parts of the world.

In the highlands of New Guinea for example, groups of people exchange shells, bird-skins and stone-axes, among many other things, at a large feast, of which the *pièce de résistance* is a pig. The 'big man's' several wives cultivate sweet potatoes to feed his pigs, which he loans out to the younger men. In this way he builds up a network of debts to be called in when he invites another 'big man' and his followers to a feast. In some tribes there is a taboo, under threat of severe ills, against eating pork if you, or a close relative, have reared it yourself. If a man is to eat pork at all he has to have fellows or partners in another group nearby with whom he can exchange pigs. The taboo has become the basis of internal order, wider peace and inter-tribal trade. The 'big man' calls in his debts at a large inter-tribal feast within which other men stage minor feasts. The guests – people who are periodically at war with their hosts – arrive dressed for the occasion and bearing gifts. During the peaceful feasting, a temporary truce, they exchange many goods. By these vitally important truces, the 'big man' in each tribe can not only secure peace by feasting with the enemy but also safeguard the internal prestige on which his influence, power and authority to settle internal tribal disputes are based. It also enables him to build up his credit of pigs. The 'big man's' reign, though ephemeral, lasts until he is too old to work or scurry about building up his network of debts; but there are some positions in the inter-tribal network that are so crucially important, that if the incumbent either dies or can no longer maintain his position, his network of relationships inside and outside the tribe must be taken over by his heir.

9

In these societies men aquire positions that are particular to them: their authority derives from their personal qualities. However, as the position of leadership can never remain unoccupied, there is a proto-office of authority to which group members may be recruited. Among the Melanesian 'big men' the rules controlling behavior are less firmly set out than among the Bushmen. They vary, as among the Eskimos, from effective but kindly leadership to outright bullying which becomes dominant in some situations. For example, when the Australian military government recaptured areas in Melanesia from the Japanese, there was a 'big man' who won their confidence, although he had previously collaborated with the enemy. He then proceeded to seize women, exploit his fellows and denounce potential rivals as collaborators themselves, until he was finally exposed by the anthropologist Hogbin. It seems that when 'big men' have been appointed by colonial powers they exploit their authority much more than if they are chosen by more traditional means.

Rule by old men or elders, gerontocracy, is a more sophisticated form of authority than that of the 'big man', although not all societies pass from one stage of development to the other. Among the Australian aborigines, who are also hunters and collectors, it is the elders who regulate marriages and have the authority to order the younger men about and settle disputes. There are also gerontocracies among pastoral people and cultivating tribes in eastern Africa in which, like the Australian Aborigines, the men undergo severe initiation rites as they are graded into 'age-sets' which span some 15 years. The age-sets are divided into youths, warriors and elders. Every 15th year there is a great ceremony at which the elders retire, the warriors become elders and can marry, and the youths become warriors with responsibility for cattle raiding and protecting the tribe. The elders of the Samburu tribe periodically repeat the symbolism of the warriors' initiation ceremony so that their acceptance of the prohibitions and abstinences required of them as warriors can be renewed. For when a warrior becomes an elder he is expected to change his behavior completely. From being exuberant, excitable and quarrelsome he must become peaceful, grave and serious; disposed to establish order rather than disorder.

The 'soldier societies' of the Cheyenne and other North American Indian tribes demanded a similar transformation of behavior when a man ceased to be a soldier and became a peace chief. The Cheyenne lived in matrilineal clans, which in the prairie winter would scatter in small bands to find shelter, and in summer reunite in one camp to hunt bison, when the men would split up and join six 'soldier societies'. In five of the societies, which would contain members from every band, the soldier chiefs acted as police and judges. They policed the bison hunt, punishing anyone who attacked the herds before the signal for general onslaught was given; they arrested and tried malefactors, and drew up legislation to meet new situations.

In the 'soldier societies', because the members were drawn from many bands, legal and moral codes are enforced and maintained by an intricate network of links and allegiances. A soldier was expected to be courageous, quick to take offence, and full of bravado. If he became too troublesome he would be tamed by being promoted to a Peace Chief and transferred to the sixth society of 44 Peace Chiefs, drawn from all the bands. The Peace Chiefs controlled the camp and cared for the sacred occult symbols of tribal unity – particularly the sanctuary of the Holy Hat and the Sacred Medicine Arrows. If one Cheyenne killed another, the Sacred Medicine Arrows were contaminated and the killer had to be expelled and the Arrows renewed – otherwise the whole earth would stink and be shunned by game.

The Sacred Arrows and the Holy Hat which were particular to the Cheyenne, are typical of a whole range of occult symbols, which sometimes included people, and on which the well-being of the tribe is believed to depend. The symbols represent the group interest in peace and prosperity which is made possible by their observance of law. The Peace Chiefs, the representatives of the symbols, derived their authority from them to enforce the law.

Relationships between groups are of key importance among societies both before and after governmental institutions have developed. Groups cannot enter into whole-hearted hostilities with each other, even if they go in for vendettas and feuds, because their members tend to be related. Marriage between close kin is forbidden among many tribes and each man or woman is related by marriage to a different group through mother, father, grandparent or child. There are always some members of a feuding group who have an interest in securing peace. Some of them, possibly related to both groups in some way, may be able to act as peacemakers and have power, if not instituted authority, to enforce the law. States where law and authority are vested in a state-governmental institution, as in western society today, were found throughout Africa and in Indonesia, and existed among the Maya, Inca and Ancient Mexicans. Here there were kings or chiefs and established offices, complete with a set of officials with accredited powers backed by police or soldiers and clearly defined functions: administrative, executive, legislative, judicial and – since the ruler often controlled the religious approach to his own ancestors or god – even ecclesiastical. However, one official might hold many offices, since the limits of authority were less clearly defined than in modern states. The states' complexity depended on technological development. There were states in which the chief and his family lived at much the same standard as the people and intermarried with them; but among the Maya, Aztec, and Inca and in parts of Africa, stone cities were built and marked the difference between ruler and subject.

In these stone cities specialized judicial courts were held. Study of these courts among the Barotse shows that they operate their courts in much the same way, although in a very different social context, as our own western courts. They listen to pleas and defenses, call witnesses, classify evidence as direct, circumstantial or hearsay. Then they convert the evidence they believe into 'facts-in-law' on which they can subsequently base their judgements using reasoning similar to that of western judges. Even in the informal courts (moots) of less institutionalized tribes similar reasoning, rules and evidence are used. Within the government organization there are struggles for control of judicial and other authority. There are tyrants as well as just rulers. Supported by police or soldiers a ruler could, if he wished, indulge in outright oppression and terror – seizing women and maiming and killing indiscriminately. But so long as there were no material means by which rulers could develop a markedly different standard of living from their subjects, these civil struggles neither took the form of outright revolution, nor aimed to change the basic organization.

Although there have been reports of struggles from West Africa, as among the Maya Indians – where they have been suggested as one probable cause of the downfall of the Maya states in the 10th century AD, and five centuries later subject people supported the invading Spaniards against their Aztec overlords – struggles for control of the state were more commonly between factions among the rulers. As in medieval England, aristocratic contenders for power would invariably put forward a member of the royal family as a leader to oust an alleged usurper or tyrant from the throne and take it over.

These civil wars, though fought in the name of kingship, were really the result of an underdeveloped and unstable economy. There was indeed some exchange of goods, and the king certainly received and distributed what the commoners paid him in taxes, but this did little to unite the factions of the polity. These aristocratic factions had no economic interdependence, no mutual treaties to bind them, and territorial autonomies developed. The people gave their loyalties to their local leaders, even to the extent of joining their private armies. Backed up by these simply-equipped armies, the chiefs made essays at power and authority, and the control of government. But the throne itself was sacrosanct, and the royal lineage, supported by occult symbols and legendary powers, was unassailable. And so the dissenter had to take as his figurehead a man of equally royal blood if he were to challenge the existing king. The affair became a genealogical wrangle. In a few West African tribes, notably the Ashanti, the movements to 'destool' (dethrone) a ruler became similar to our legal actions, as ritual was invoked to plead the case. Such actions became more and more frequent under colonial rule, as contending factions tried to manipulate their European governors in the disputes.

11

Peoples of the Caribbean

One of the outstanding facts about the Caribbean is that it is an area populated almost totally by immigrants. The landfall of Columbus at San Salvador (Watling Island) in the Bahamas in 1492 precipitated a flow of peoples from the Old World to the New which has not yet ceased. In the Caribbean, societies have been created whose major characteristic is ethnic diversity. Today there are three major racial components in the Caribbean: the African, the European and, to a smaller extent, the element from the sub-continent of India. With these are associated a number of minority groups such as the Chinese, people of mixed African and European descent, and the Lebanese. All are descended from immigrant groups which arrived at different periods in the history of the islands.

The Spaniards, however, the first European settlers, did not arrive to find a population vacuum. At the end of the 15th and the early 16th century, the West Indies were inhabited by three major groups of Amerindians: Arawaks, Caribs and Tanala. Today, except for a remnant in Dominica, these peoples have ceased to exist. Their extinction was the result of the Spaniards' policies of enslavement in gold mines and on the land, the warfare which developed from resistance to slavery, and dispossession of Amerindian lands. The destruction of these people was completed by the introduction of diseases from Europe. Reliable historical sources suggest that in 1492 the population of Hispaniola – the modern Haiti and Dominican Republic – was between 200,000 and 300,000. By 1510 there were only 46,000. Four years later only 14,000 remained.

The Spanish crown can only indirectly be blamed for this genocide. There were regulations to safeguard the Indian. But the system of *encomienda*, by which the Amerindians were given in trust to the colonists, was abused from the beginning by the ruthless rapacity of the colonists, beyond the control of a government 4,000 miles away. The destruction of the aborigines was inevitable.

As is usual, attempts were made to justify this systematic exploitation. The rationalizations have a familiar ring: '. . . they eat human flesh. They are more given to sodomy than any other nation. There is no justice among them. They go naked. . . . They are ungrateful and changeable. . . . Traitorous, cruel and vindictive. . . . I may affirm that God has never created a race more full of vice and composed without the least mixture of kindness or culture . . .'

The Spaniards were forced by the depletion of the Amerindian labor force and the gradual change from abortive gold mining to a plantation economy, to look to other sources of labor. As early as 1497 they had tried importing Spanish convict labor from Europe. It remained a unique experiment. It was not Spain but Britain, France and Holland who adopted the policy of sending to the Caribbean male and female criminals, political prisoners and vagabonds, as well as those cajoled and kidnapped as indentured labor.

Indentured labor or bonded servitude was a form of quasi-slavery used all over the Americas, except in the Spanish domains, during the colonial period. The individual was bound by his articles of indenture to serve for a number of years – generally four. If he was insubordinate his master could extend the term. And the indentured worker could be passed from one master to another by the sale of his indentures. His predicament was if anything worse than that of the negro slave.

As the West Indies were opened up by colonial powers other than Spain in the 17th century the settlers owned large tracts of land and a class of planters with pretensions to gentility developed throughout the islands. In 1664 the Council for Foreign Plantations noted that indentured servants were largely '. . . felons condemned to death, sturdy beggars, gypsies, and other incorrigible rogues, poor and idle debauched persons. . . .' Few returned home after their indenture was finished. Some were lucky enough to acquire land and set up as planters. But the majority appear not to have risen above the level of subsistence farming.

The descendants of white indentured laborers have remained distinct in the European population of the Caribbean. Their poverty has barred them from intercourse with the white 'establishment' in the islands. Anxiety to preserve their color has led to inbreeding. Their way of life is not significantly different from the surrounding black peasantry. People of African descent despise them for not fulfilling the stereotype of white superiority. The formerly dominant white group reject them as people who tarnish the white man's image. The poor whites represent the failure of European colonization in the West Indies. To ascertain their actual number is difficult as they are not separately classified in censuses. But they survive on several islands.

The main region of Africa from which slaves were drawn is bounded by Senegal in the north and Angola in the south. Some few thousands of slaves came from East Africa and Madagascar but the trade can be considered virtually a West African phenomenon. It is important to realize that slavery itself was endemic in Africa at this time. The European used this 'domestic' slavery as a basis for building the vast and lucrative economic structure of plantation slavery. Initially Africans sold for transportation across the Atlantic were captives taken in local wars. As the demand grew, specific slave-raiding expeditions were organized by Africans with the assistance of Europeans and Arabs.

The conditions under which the 'Middle Passage' was attempted were terrifying. According to evidence given in the British House of Commons in 1791 'Mr Falconbridge also states in this head, that when employed in stowing the slaves he made the most of the room and wedged them in. They had not so much room as a man in his coffin either in length or breadth.' It is not surprising that in such conditions, on a voyage which lasted weeks, the mortality rate was extremely high. '. . . Mr Morley says, that in four voyages he purchased about 1325, and lost about 132. . . . The surgeon of the *Hero* told him, that when the slaves were moved from one place to another, they left the marks of their skin and blood upon the deck, and it was the most horrid sight that he had even seen. . . . Captain Hall in two voyages purchased 550, and lost 110. He adds, that he has known some ships in the slave trade bury a quarter, some a third, and others half of their cargo. . . . .'

No attempt was made to keep families or people from the same tribe together. The separation of families was simple cruelty. The dissolution of tribal communities made it easier to control the slave on the sugar estate. The African was obliged to learn the language of his new masters – French, Dutch, British or Spanish – not only for communication between slave-owner and slave, but also between slave and slave.

Deprived of freedom, forced to labor in the fields, and unable to communicate in his mother tongue it was not surprising that the slave lost the greater part of his African culture. Traces of this remain only in areas least susceptible to the planter's control, such as magic and religion. The island in which this is most prominent is Haiti. The contribution of the African to Caribbean society should be seen more in terms of the creolization of the negro, through his experience of slavery and his sojourn in the islands, than in terms of his African legacy.

Slavery for the negro meant not only that his liberty was denied; it meant entry into a world of profound cruelty. 'Mr Dalrymple, in June 1789, saw a negress brought to St George's, Grenada, to have her fingers cut off. She had committed a fault, and run away to avoid punishment; but being taken, her master suspended her by the hands, flogged and cut her cruelly on the back, belly, breast, and thighs, and then left her suspended until her fingers mortified. In this state Mr Dalrymple saw her at Dr Gilpin's house. . .'
to General Frere at an estate of his in Barbados, and riding one morning with the General and two other officers, they saw near a house, upon a dunghill, a naked negro nearly suspended, by strings from his elbows backward, to the bough of a tree, with his feet barely upon the ground, and an iron weight round his neck, at least to appearance of 14 lb. weight: and thus without one creature near him, or apparently near the house, was this wretch left exposed to the noon-day sun. Returning a few hours after, they found him still in the same state, and would have released him, but for the advice of General Frere, who had an estate in the neighborhood. . . .'

Although in theory they were governed by slave codes promulgated by the metropolitan governments 4,000 miles away, planters on their West Indian estates felt free to administer punishment as they thought fit. Towards the slave they were cruel, but they were capable of the most tender affection for their own families. Like the white indentured servant, the slave was possibly not regarded as a human being. Tender feelings were reserved for one's own kind. The rest were merely recalcitrant animals. The historical process which we call creolization affected both master and slave. The contemporary Caribbean white is more West Indian than he is anything else. His ancestors could afford to indulge in cruelty even if it resulted in the death of the slave, who was replaceable.

Creolization has bonded black and white together in a number of contradictory ways, partly because miscegenation has created a mixed or colored group. These *gens de couleur* have played a significant role in the development of West Indies society. White men found concubines among the African women: their offspring were more privileged than the majority of slaves. If they were not freed they were given the lighter household tasks rather than the onerous labor of the field slave. As the process continued colored rather than black women became white men's concubines and so were created the many color gradations in the Caribbean today.

Manumission was the right of the slave owner to free his slaves, particularly at a planter's death-bed when he could not contemplate the return of his concubine and their children to the status of true slaves after his death. Many inherited property and money from their master-father, in some islands to such an extent that laws were passed to limit the amount.

Despite his privileges the free colored man knew that he was not and never could be accepted by white society. Yet he was willing and eager to attach himself to the white establishment, the source of power and authority. In education and social behavior, the colored man had nothing in common with the black slave. He resented the color he had inherited which prevented him from becoming totally identified with the white group. The *gens de couleur* were willing mediators in the conflicts between black and white before and after the emancipation of the slaves. In the 19th century many were honoured and rose to high office in the different colonies' forming an aristocracy parallel with that of the whites.

Throughout the period of slavery the European population in the Caribbean varied from the poor whites to the aristocracy. A minority were scions of distinguished families who set out for the Indies to make their fortune, and in many instances succeeded. Others were of humbler origin. Foot soldiers, for example, were granted land in the newly conquered colony after a successful campaign there. In Jamaica a number of distinguished white families owe their fortune to ancestors who were rewarded for fighting in the victorious army of Penn and Venables against the Spaniards in 1655. The new land-owners acquired gentility in the fullness of time.

The abolition of slavery in the British Caribbean in 1834, and in the French possessions in 1848, was a 13 turning point in West Indian history. It was the beginning of an era when new elements would be added to the already heterogeneous population. Freed slaves were reluctant to work for wages on the sugar estates. To offset the new shortage of workers, local governments sought permission from the national governments to import indentured labor from other parts of the world.

The main immigrant contribution was to come from Asia – from India and Hong Kong. Nearly half a million east Indians came to the Caribbean between 1838 and 1917; initially they were brought in as indentured labor. The east Indian in creole society has attempted to resist creolization by marrying his own kind, adhering to Hinduism or Islam, and to a lesser extent by preserving his Indian mother tongue. But there has been a steady cultural erosion and the present young generation of east Indians in the Caribbean feel themselves more West Indian than anything else. Endogamy – marrying your own kind – tends to be strong where there is a substantial Indian population, as in Trinidad, but where the east Indian group is smaller, as in Jamaica, there are as many creoles as there are Indians. The 20th century east Indian in the Caribbean is no longer an indentured laborer, but is still largely associated with agriculture. A substantial minority in Trinidad, but a smaller number in Jamaica, has entered the professions, commerce and a number of trades.

The pattern of Chinese immigration was different. The flow of indentured agricultural labor for the plantations from Hong Kong began in the 1850s and continued almost to the end of the 19th century. During this period there were over 20,000 immigrants who went mainly to Guyana, Trinidad and Jamaica. Their association with the land was brief. Today it is exceptional to find a Chinese working on the land. They are all in some way involved in trading or commerce either in a village grocery shop, or in a large commercial combine.

The immigration of the Portuguese to the West Indies was exceptional. They came not from Portugal, but from Madeira and the Azores between 1835 and the end of the 19th century and in some parts of the West Indies, notably Guyana – where they form a separate category – they are not regarded as European in the same sense as the Anglo-Saxons. Nearly 40,000 probably came as indentured laborers. Like the Chinese their involvement with the land was nominal and only preceded their entry into trading and commerce. As most West Indian census data classifies them as 'white' and they have intermarried, it is difficult to determine their numbers.

One vital element in the racial composition of the Caribbean is the Syrians and the Lebanese. They appear to have come to the islands first as visitors, notably to the Jamaica Exhibition of 1891. The visitors gave way to peddlers and traveling hucksters. Today the tiny Lebanese minority plays a role in the commercial life of the Caribbean out of all proportion to its numbers.

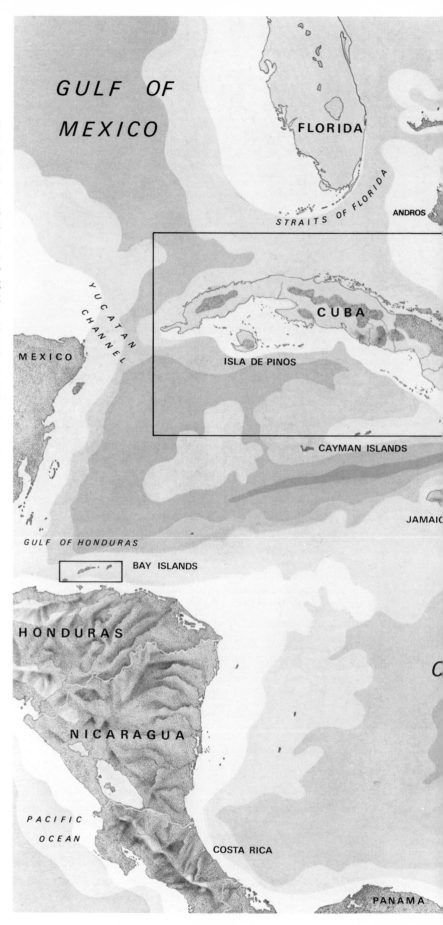

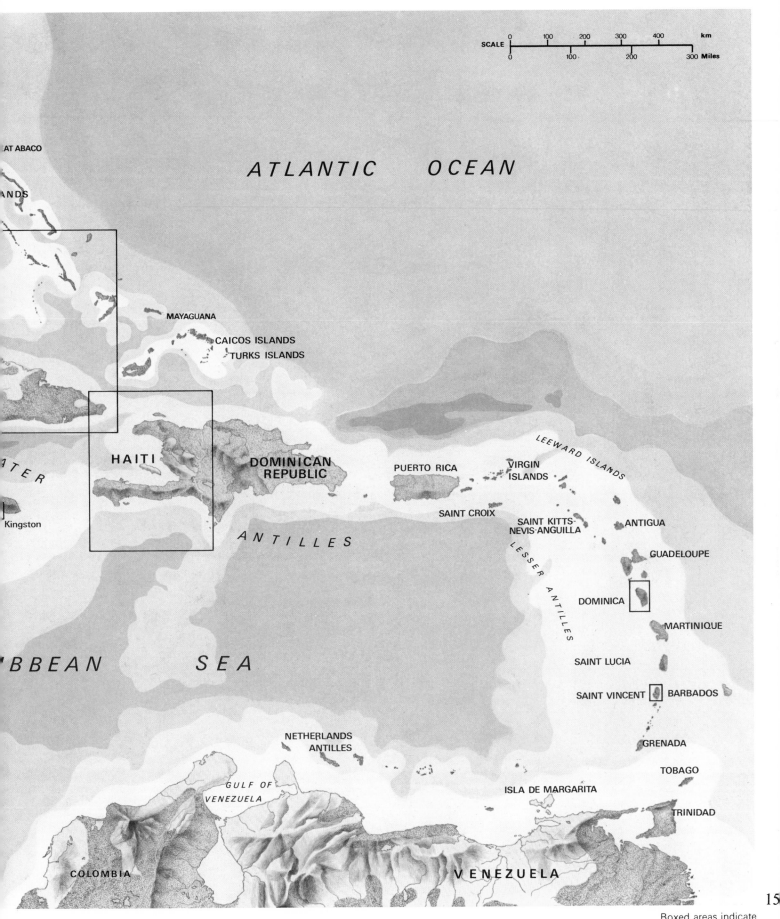

ATLANTIC OCEAN

AT ABACO

NDS

MAYAGUANA

CAICOS ISLANDS
TURKS ISLANDS

LEEWARD ISLANDS

ATER

HAITI

DOMINICAN
REPUBLIC

PUERTO RICA

VIRGIN
ISLANDS

Kingston

SAINT CROIX

ANTIGUA

ANTILLES

SAINT KITTS-
NEVIS-ANGUILLA

GUADELOUPE

LESSER ANTILLES

DOMINICA

MARTINIQUE

BBEAN   SEA

SAINT LUCIA

SAINT VINCENT   BARBADOS

NETHERLANDS
ANTILLES

GRENADA

TOBAGO

GULF OF
VENEZUELA

ISLA DE MARGARITA

TRINIDAD

COLOMBIA

VENEZUELA

SCALE
0   100   200   300   400   km
0   100   200   300 Miles

15

Boxed areas indicate
peoples discussed in
this volume.

The Cubans

Once a Spanish colony, Cuba
is now one of the world's
more austere socialistic
states. But some comrades
smoke its famous cigars.

6

Cuba, seen from the skies, is green and pleasant, in splendid contrast to the drab, exhausted colors of much of the Caribbean area. This verdure springs from its immensely fertile soil, the presence everywhere of water, and the forests that still cover a quarter of its total area. Throughout its history since it was settled, its resources have been conserved by great landowners who spared no effort in the efficient production of sugar. Emancipation from slavery was followed by over-population, soil-exhaustion and destitution in islands such as Haiti; but the great estates of Cuba remained undivided and profitably run for the benefit of a tiny handful of Cubans. The high prices from their crop had enabled the sugar barons to buy the finest equipment – and the most vigorous and handsome slaves. The latter factor encouraged inter-marriage and concubinage. A high proportion of Cubans have a slave ancestress somewhere in the family tree, and this judicious admixture has contributed to the extraordinary good looks of the population.

The slave trade persisted for decades after its legal abolition, provoking international scandal and many admonitions from the Spanish Crown to their captains general. The latter acted with extreme discretion knowing that to drive the powerful sugar barons too far would only have provoked secession to the US. These slave-owning planters were unpatriotic and hugely prosperous, and the benign and helpful attitude of the northern capitalists – as opposed to the pettyfogging Spanish legalism under which they suffered – attracted rich Cubans to the idea of annexation.

Many Americans were in enthusiastic agreement with them, and an invasion was actually planned as early as 1854, though nothing came of it. A new mood of expansionism began to prevail in 1890, after the massacre of Wounded Knee. The conquest of territory in the far west had come to an end, so the expansionists were obliged to look south. The moment seemed happily to coincide with a time when Spain's hold on its last colonial possessions was at its weakest.

For several years there had been guerilla warfare in Cuba between the forces of the Spanish Crown and Cuban insurgents. By the spring of 1898 a military stalemate had been reached. Fighting had ceased and the two sides seemed perilously near coming to terms.

At this point the US interventionists, led by William Randolph Hearst, father of yellow journalism, went into action. Hearst called on the people of the United States not to shirk even the ultimate sacrifice of war in defense of the downtrodden Cubans. He sent correspondents to Cuba with instructions to manufacture atrocity stories. When one of them cabled, 'Everything is quiet. There is no trouble here. There will be no war' Hearst replied 'You furnish the pictures and I'll furnish the war.' The war was furnished, Spain collapsed, and Cuba emerged virtually as a US protectorate. A tight control 17

Marxist severity has not
quite extinguished the
Cubans' innate gusto and
haphazard improvization in
their city dwellings.

was preferred to the outright annexation called for by so many. A great deal of the national wealth changed hands by methods that did not exclude chicanery and gangsterism. The United Fruit Company was allowed to buy the island's most fertile land at $2 per acre and the superb harbor of Guantanamo, with 45 square miles of surrounding land, was leased in perpetuity for $2,000 per annum. The Platt Amendment, written into the constitution, permitted the US to land troops and take over the island almost at will.

There were the unpromising circumstances attending the birth of modern Cuba. It was to remain without industries, entirely dependent upon sugar – and as the cultivation of sugar cane calls only for short and sporadic employment, almost the whole male population

Cubans love sport. These days they are determined to excel internationally — and there are Soviet instructors to help them.

18

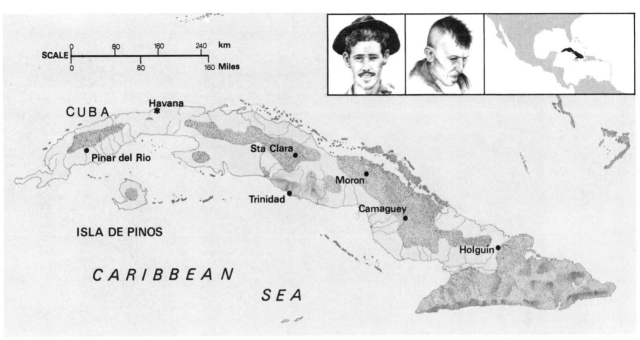

A white wedding in red Havana,
where atheistic Marxism has
joined hands with formerly
inflexible Catholicism in a
newly declared friendship.

19

Statistics show production
results (in white) even
higher than the planned
output (in black). It is
hard to check the accuracy.

A Castro quote above a bus
stop: 'In the past we queued
to identify cousins killed or
tortured; now we stand in
line to buy bread.

of the island was, in effect, out of work for nine months out of twelve. Superficially, it remained a gay country. Much of the Cuban's enormous leisure was spent in amusing himself as best he could, at fiestas, cock-fighting bouts, rustic bull-fights and rodeos, dancing and singing, and in the creation of a wealth of charming popular music: the *habaneras, guajiras*, and *milongas* which combined the Moorish music of southern Spain with the rhythm of African drums; and *romanzos*, the witty vocalized extemporizations which recalled the Jamaican calypso. Every second man played a musical instrument, and the carnival of Havana was only sur-passed anywhere in zest and color by that of Rio. No equivalent of the melancholic negro-spirituals and work songs exists in Cuban folk music.

A quarter of the population of about 7 million were either negroes or mulattos, and although no color bar officially existed, in practice the races remained sep-arated. Colored Cubans performed menial labor, were more prolific, and suffered from higher rates of infant mortality, sickness and illiteracy. As elsewhere in the West Indies, colored family ties were looser than those among whites. Slavery in Cuba had been mild in character by comparison with the forms practised else-where, and a system called *coartación* permitted a high proportion of slaves to purchase their freedom by instalments. However, slavery split up families and left its legacy of parental irresponsibility. Negro fathers came and went, and still do, with small regard for the obligations of paternity. Many colored Cuban children have in effect been orphaned by a system which has long ceased to exist. Two-thirds of the rural population lived in *bohios* – palm-thatched huts, usually consisting of a single room – in which numerous families were often reared. Even so, the characteristic Cuban gaiety remained unaffected by empty stomachs.

Throughout most of this century Cubans have got poorer as the value of sugar has fallen in relation to that of imported goods. In 1956, at a time when it was said that there were more Cadillacs on the streets of Havana than any other city in the world, the Catholic University Students' Association published statistics showing that only one Cuban in a hundred ate fish, only two could afford an occasional egg, and only four ever ate meat. Rice and beans – 'Christians and Moors' – was, at it still is, their basic diet.

The hold of Christianity has always been weak in country parts – weaker than anywhere else in Latin America – particularly in the east of the island, where many African cults exist: some of them like the santerias devoted to innocent mumbo-jumbo – others, such as the nañigos, more sinister, and involving the sacrifice of cocks and goats and at one time, a half-century ago, of human beings too.

The voodoo practices of Cuba have remained closer to African models, even than those of Haiti, and many of

21

Work is tough in this
refinery pressing plant:
the factory was confiscated
from a US firm, but it now
desperately lacks spares.

the gods of the African pantheon, such as Yoruba, god of lightning and storms, and Chango, the war-god, continue to be revered under their old names. The rituals associated with these cults remain on the whole authentic. In the early part of this century, several thousand Cuban negroes were still alive who had actually been born in Africa, and in some cases they could remember the rituals. This did not prevent the subsequent adoption of many Christian saints and their identification with the African gods. St Peter was identified with Elegua, master of the Paths, St Francis had become the African Crumila (Destiny), and St John the Baptist – as in Haiti – became Ogun, a war god with a partiality to strong liquor, whose initiates drink huge potions of rum mixed with red pepper, without becoming noticeably drunk. Most original and interesting of the cults is that of the Abakua, a unique example of an African bush society transported intact from its homeland in Nigeria to the New World. The mysteries of this cult – its devotees are the Nañigos. – have never been fully penetrated by an outsider, but its central theme is reported as a belief in reincarnation. This is to be avoided where possible, and there are mystic practices which permit the soul to enter an African version of Nirvana.

The pseudo-African religious scene of Cuba has been complicated by a large number of Haitian immigrant workers, who brought with them many of the innumerable Haitian cults. These have been treated with some reserve by the black Cuban peasantry, much impressed by accounts of the occult powers of their. *bokors* – in particular their ability to create zombies by resurrecting corpses and holding them in mindless servitude through the practice of black magic.

These African cults have not been exclusive to negroes and mulattos. By the middle of the present century a growing section of the white population was being attracted away from the disciplines of the Catholic Church by the emotionalism and the excitements of the jungle religions. The Nañigos resolutely barred such would-be converts, but such was their prestige that a white sect was formed which imitated their rituals and sacrifices in so far as they were known. It was considered smart to join an African cult. St Barbara, a Christianized African goddess, sometimes known as the spirit of the Ceiba tree, was favored by the sophisticates of Havana, who worked themselves into a frenzy at her shrine, and smeared a little cock's blood on their faces. It was reported around the time Castro came to power (1959) that almost as many middle-class whites of Havana visited St Barbara's shrines as went to church, and the local Woolworth's had several counters displaying her cult objects. So benevolent was Cuban officialdom's attitude toward the religions of Africa that one of the last acts of the dictator Batista before he fled the country in 1959 was to summon to the capital and pay out of his own pocket for a convention of voodoo

Workers cut cane in Las Villas. Despite grandiose co-operative diversification schemes, sugar is still the base of Cuban economy.

A cemetery houses nominal
Christians. But even the
white middle class divides
its allegiance between
Christianity and voodoo.

Thatching skill — a legacy
of African village life —
persists in country areas.
Almost every Cuban has a
black slave ancestor.

23

Cuba's leader Fidel Castro
rarely quotes the little Marx
he has read. But he claims to
follow Marx and Lenin – and
shops sell their busts.

priests. There is no evidence that the present Marxist regime is actively suppressing these cults; but it seems likely that the spread of education, and the association of the cults, in the minds of the young, with a decadent past will bring about their inevitable decline.

The period between the Spanish American War and Castro's coming to power was one of spectacular corruption. In the 1930s, for example, José Manuel Alemán, the Minister of Education, arrived one day at the treasury with three lorries into which he and his retainers stuffed the whole of the Cuban cash reserves, after which the loot was transferred to Alemán's yacht, and Alemán departed for Miami. A private suit for 174 million dollars – brought against him as a result of this – failed. Alemán had bought off all the opposition. The strange thing was that nobody seemed to think much the worse of him. He won a reputation for generosity, largely based on his habit of finding some excuse to present any perfect stranger he happened to meet casually with a thousand dollar bill. Alemán died peacefully and fairly well respected in a Havana nursing home.

A more characteristic coup was the sale by the head of the Public Health Department of five million dollars' worth of medical supplies (including all the blankets) looted from Havana hospitals. During this period

24

One of thousands of Russian
technicians stumblingly
teaches a Cuban welder. Few
speak Spanish: temperaments
are different too.

elections were a farce. In 1939 in the Parque Centrál, a politician machine-gunned down a number of unemployed men who had formed a ring to extort the sum of 1 peso 25 cents per vote, instead of the 1 peso habitually paid. By 1953, American gangsters had moved in to control the gambling casinos for which the city was famous, and Lucky Luciano had arrived from Naples to set up his headquarters for the world traffic in narcotics. By now Cuba was one of the most corrupt countries in the world: the 'brothel' for the eastern seaboard of the US, Havana was the Fun City of the western world to which New Yorkers flocked for divorces, abortions and sexual extravagances. Then on 1 January 1959, Fidel Castro and his revolutionary band came down from the mountains with the intention of restoring his country's lost esteem. Batista, last and worst of the dictators, fled the country, and an era was at an end.

In October 1958 the leaders of the new government, who were at that time still in hiding in the mountains, 'decreed' a reform by which 100,000 sharecropper tenants and squatters were to be given the 150 or so acres of land that each of them worked. It could have been implemented almost anywhere else in Latin America, in any country where the great landed estates remained in national hands. But 40 per cent of Cuban land, as well as most of the public utilities, was owned by North American companies. The Castro government could therefore make no move without damaging Cuba's foreign interests, and eventually provoked a furious counter-attack. The Cuban land reforms were cautious and partial by Communist standards, and hardly more stringent than those enacted in post-war Japan by General MacArthur, but the cry went up that Castro was a Communist. Castro endorsed the accusation himself; and a series of economic sanctions were planned. US credits to Cuba were cut off, and a Cuban attempt to raise a loan in Europe was blocked. The USSR was, predictably, ready to step in as the economic savior. Cuba has subsequently undergone the improbable transformation into a Communist state. Improbable, since traditionally, despite their hardships and the inequities of their lives, Cubans have been the gayest and most carefree of Caribbean peoples. These national characteristics are not extinguished. But there are marked changes; how profound only time will tell.

In the first place, they have lost the whole of the landed class (with a handful of exceptions, including Fidel Castro himself), virtually the entire middle class, and a significant proportion of the artisan class. Over a million citizens, more than one-seventh of the population, 'voted with their feet,' as Lenin would say, and left the country. Engineers and doctors, teachers and lawyers, businessmen and managers, quit in their thousands with their families, leaving behind them everything they possessed. They poured into Florida, Mexico and Central America, to start life again, sometimes to plot their return – more than ten years later, most retain a determination to go back. Some, the more recalcitrant or the political suspects, went as Castro's prisoners to the Isla de Pinos, Cuba's southern satellite isle. Almost all those who have left Cuba have been white or predominantly so: the traditional racial balance has thus markedly changed in a few years – although it is noticeable that political authority is still overwhelmingly in white hands. And into Cuba have come several thousand (pale) Russians, as political advisers; civil servants, indoctrinators, technicians and even sports instructors.

To the Russians, Cuba is a much sought-after posting. For although so severe and strange an ideology has had a markedly desiccating effect on the personality of many of the Cuban servants of the new regime, Cuban gusto and *joie de vivre* are still evident. Skirts in Havana are still the tightest in the world (to the disgust of certain of the more matronly Soviet wives); there is still something of the old swagger to life, especially among the soldiery, in the image of Fidel's romantic guerrilla force. The grand plans for diversifying agriculture have not

A militia woman sits by a shop window. Cuba has a war-time economy: queues are long, goods are rationed and shop windows are half-filled.

8 3155

25

Most Cuban women serve for
a time in the army or militia.
Despite intense tuition,
they generally turn out to
be poor shots.

Cuban enthusiasm for
Marxismo-Leninismo is
coupled with strict
discipline for the swelling
number of schoolchildren

(Top) Marching schoolgirls
join the struggle to change
Cuba's image from one of
sybaritic decadence into one
of organizational fervor.

(Bottom) The peasants and
cane cutters can be grateful
for a new dignity. Yet only
time will tell whether the
revolution will 'stick.'

worked out: Cuba has been compelled to fall back on sugar which represents 80 per cent of her exports. Appalling administrative malfunctions still dog the system: in the early years of Castro's regime, thousands of peasants were set to work to reclaim scrub-land, but much of this remained unplanted, and the new acres vanished from sight. In an export-at-all-costs drive, eggs were sent by the million to Venezuela, leaving not enough for the Cuban hatcheries to carry on. Tomatoes were shipped at great expense to Canada, where the market promptly expired as the US sold at a loss to undercut Cuban prices. The few fishermen who did not decamp to Miami seemed only to catch hake. But nearly all the *bohios* have gone, and so have the city-edge squatter settlements, and in their place, neat little three room government dwellings with concrete floors, decorated with little flags saying *Gracias a Fidel* and sometimes with pictures of Lenin or the Virgin and sometimes both. And there is *alfabetismo* for all, young and old, a higher proportion of money being spent on (Marxist) education than anywhere in Latin America. Crime is low (the penalties being severe), exhortation is everywhere. And there is, at the top, the vividly Cuban figure of Fidel Castro himself – energectic, erratic, full of charisma,

garrulous, daring, injudicious, benign and bullying.

Despite the totality of state ownership, on the Russian pattern, the more sophisticated of Cubans still on their island have been heard to speculate on how long the ideology will prevail once the US blockade is lifted. For although gratitude is genuine for the disappearance of real poverty and of the shanty-towns so familiar in the Latin American scene, for universal schooling and care of the children, there is no sign yet of the elimination of the queue, most foods are rationed (even sugar and cigars), and Cubans continue to endure a war-time economy. Cubans are still far from the presumption that life ought to be austere. In the grandiose towers that once were American hotels, the air-conditioning has long ceased, the elevators are unreliable, and the food dismal; the party meetings in the foyer are attended only by the ambitious. Meanwhile the Catholic Church is keeping its end up. Several bishops were among the early friends of the revolution, and the Government is smart enough to encourage this young element in the priesthood that has convinced itself that atheistic Marxism is compatible with Christianity. Weekly columns are devoted to religious news in the government controlled press. It does not happen in Pravda.

Trinidadians and Carnival

In a frenzy of noisy and
garish exuberance that lasts
two days and nights, Carnival
purges Trinidadians of a
whole year's pent-up emotion.

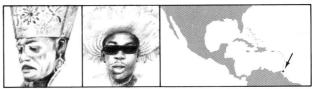

Nobody within miles of Port-of-Spain, Trinidad's capital, gets much sleep on the night of the last Sunday before Lent. Elderly tourists, who swarm to the island all the rest of the year, are warned away. Soon after midnight the hubbub begins. At first only the occasional distant make-shift drum crashes. As the small hours of morning creep in, late stayers decide to drink on till dawn. 'You can't go to bed now, man – it's only two hours till Jour Ouvert.' Disjointed sounds follow each other more and more frequently. Slowly the air seems to fill with the reverberation of some massive orchestra tuning up, its many varied instruments miles apart from each other – until, well before dawn has broken, the whole city and countryside around are awake to the rowdy, exuberant, extravagant sounds that proclaim the beginning of Carnival.

For two days the drumming never stops. Tuesday – Mardi Gras or Shrove Tuesday – is the big day, the climax of the show, when the place boils over with excitement. It is the day when the huge bands – some a thousand strong – parade through the streets and down to the Savannah Racecourse where they compete against each other for the vaunted title of Band of the Year.

But on Monday excitement is already bubbling in the streets which soon thicken with hundreds of garishly dressed celebrants outdoing each other in noise and dance. Observers look for hints of what is coming on the next day. Bandsmen flaunt themselves in small groups and in ones and twos, while onlookers try to work out which band is dressing in what style, whose band is going to be the biggest, who is impersonating whom.

Everyone in the streets soon succumbs to the relentless and irresistibly drugging haunt of the rhythms. Everyone joins the swell of jigging, prancing, whooping humanity. Everyone is swept away in the sea of frenzied jubilation that swirls over the city. Many watchers, detached one moment, are physically swept away the next, by waves of enthusiastic Carnival masqueraders.

Tuesday is the great day. In front of the racecourse grandstand a vast stage, over a hundred yards long, awaits the contestant bands. All afternoon the parade continues. The biggest bands take half an hour to march past. Band leaders are easy to pick out – tense with pride and expectation. The final glorious moments when they take the stage, with their hordes of loyal followers tumbling behind them, are the results of months of arrangement and research. The bands' dress must be accurate as well as eye-catching.

Biblical events are often depicted – Joshua and the 2

A band may number a
thousand, every member
painted and dressed
identically. This man
is in a 'Papuan war band'

crumbling walls of Jericho, Moses leading his people out of Egypt, scenes from English history, Alexander and his conquering army, the Crusades. A recent winner enacted Caesar's·conquest of Gaul – the band leader was of course Caesar himself. He had cunningly chosen this because Caesar's Gallic wars were the basic Latin text in all the elementary schools that year. Phalanx after phalanx of legionaries clanked past, breastplates glittering in the scorching heat, tawny faces of the soldiers intent. Brown vestal virgins skipped by, swinging smoking censers; trumpeters lifted long, dazzlingly gilded horns; standard bearers hoisted tinkling metal trees of trophies emblazoned SPQR. Then, behind his generals, strode Caesar himself – and behind him the captive barbarians of Gaul. It was *Ben Hur*, *Spartacus*, all Trinidad's favorite Hollywood epics rolled into one.

The assault of noise and color upon the ears and eyes is stupendous. Every year the bands get bigger. Nowadays there are no sections of society that stand aloof. But the announcement of the arrival of the band from Maraval is still greeted with as much disbelief as fascination by the gigantic audience. For Maraval – a long, enclosed valley running north from the city – is the white suburb of Port-of-Spain. Its Country Club, last bastion of white supremacy, had been an object of myth and detestation for many people of Trinidad until Independence in 1962. During World War II, when hundreds of British and American servicemen were given temporary membership, its color bar on guests was slightly relaxed. Yet the legend ran round Port-of-Spain that a pale brown paper-bag was hung by the front door, and no lady of darker pigmentation was allowed to pass it. Few of today's Maraval band would fail the paperbag test. But Carnival has captured the whole island – and since Independence has become the symbol of unity.

Towards the end of the day, eyes glaze with fatigue, legs want to give way, dancers leap lower, and movements become mechanical. An 'Indian brave' collapses in the sidewalk; a 'US marine' slumps in someone else's front garden. But almost island-wide catharsis has been achieved – the pent-up feelings of a whole year have been joyously released in a couple of days. About 100,000 people live in Port-of-Spain – and a good 50,000 of them cross that judging stage at Carnival-time.

Far from being the cement of Trinidad society that Carnival is today, it was once shunned, despised and even feared by all except those who themselves took part. The deepest roots of Carnival go back to the orgiastic masquerades of the Roman Bacchanalia and Saturnalia. The Popes of Rome themselves indulged in the three day 'farewell to meat' that in effect meant a bout of eating and drinking of the grossest and most extravagant kind.

In Trinidad the creoles were the creators of today's Carnival. Descendants of negro slaves and Frenchmen – and therefore Catholic – they transformed Carnival from a genteel and coquettish diversion of the Catholic upper

A 'robber' in traditional sequined trousers and huge fringed wedding-cake hat stalks the festive streets terrorizing small boys.

classes into a vibrant folk festival in which the participants could purge themselves of emotions held in check for the rest of the year. In 1834 slavery in Trinidad was abolished and the newly freed slaves also began to develop their own rousing Carnival.

Before the negroes and creoles revolutionized Carnival, they had already won a reputation among the whites for irreverence and unbridled rowdiness by their nightlong wakes which marked any death in their communities. Death for whites in Trinidad meant a hastily arranged funeral and private grief among the bereaved. But among those of African descent, death reminded all of the indissoluble link between the living, the dead, and members of the family yet to be born. The night-long wakes were not merely a public demonstration of sorrow on the part of the next of kin, but also times for drink, dance and music. The belief in *obeah* or sorcery was widespread among negroes and creoles throughout the 19th century – and this too was condemned by the whites, though according to the famous governor Lord Harris many whites themselves made use of *obeah*, so perhaps there was an element of envy in their haughty scoffing at negro practices. However, negroes and creoles were undeterred by the dis- 31

This celebrant carries a conventional – if home-made – harp. But instruments range from biscuit-tins to garbage can lids and 44-gallon drums.

approval of others, and brought the rhythms and riches of Africa to enliven traditional European Catholic ritual. Moreover the upper classes of Trinidad were mainly Protestant. To them, Carnival – let alone Carnival embellished by the creoles with the paraphernalia of 'savage' Africa – was foreign, and reeked of France.

Masking was singled out for criticism by the upright – for it too spoke of foreign licentiousness. Even the Governor was scolded in 1842 for holding a masked ball. But for the creoles, masks were an essential part of Carnival garb. In 1846 when it was forbidden to wear masks outdoors, false beards and spectacles served the same purpose. Masks were by no means new to the slaves. Many of the forest peoples of West Africa – for example the Kono of Guinea – wore masks if they held prominent positions in rituals.

Masks were no doubt useful for those who wished to commit excesses without being recognized. Scores could be paid off against enemies. Liberties are often taken by Carnival merrymakers because nobody knows who they are. A 'robber' in traditional sequinned trousers hides his identity under a huge fringed wedding-cake hat. He stalks through the streets terrorizing small boys. Other 'robbers' with heads under stockings stop passers-by – who hopefully presume the 'robber' is jesting – and demand 'money or your life'. Hooded 'vampire bats' swoop at you flapping their wings and veering off just in time, or accost pretty girls and make outrageous proposals in monstrous voices. But the wearing of masks – apart from the sheer fun of it – touches the very core of the festival's deeper meaning.

Carnival turns everything upside down – metaphorically speaking as a rule, but sometimes literally too. You are no longer yourself. A large section of society denied a voice suddenly finds one – and discovers that it is the loudest on the island. A people who can barely remember their own African past take over the history of their oppressors and make it their own. A people who visibly wear the scars of slavery treat their former masters with familiarity. A poverty-stricken and humiliated people find unity and pride amongst themselves to belie Lord Harris's sorrowful pronouncement that 'a race had been freed but a society not yet born'. That society takes firm shape for a couple of days – and it is a society of kings.

But Carnival is not merely escapism. There are direct social references, often critical in many of the favorite 'acts'. For example, the popularity of 'vampire bats' derives from the rabies scare of the 1930s. 'Canboulay' – originally *cannes brûlées* (burnt canes) – gleefully recalls an exciting plantation fire of over a hundred years ago. Celebrants carry torches which they sometimes flail against each other.

Caricaturing the island's establishment leaders has been a favorite part of Carnival for over a century. In 1866 a recent murder trial in the Supreme Criminal court was mercilessly parodied; even the gestures of the

To be Queen of a band is a dream come true for the girls of Trinidad. The dazzling and elaborate costume may cost $300.

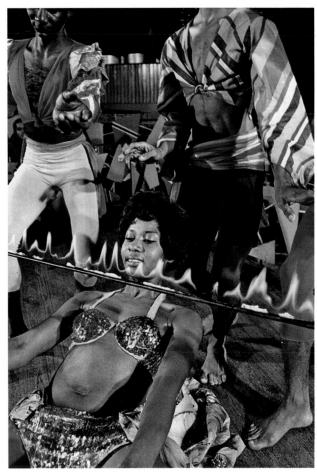

learned Attorney-General, complete with wig and gown, were mimicked. Unsuccessful cricket teams often come in for derisive laughter, and each individual team-member is lampooned. Curiously enough, the whites apparently enjoyed this aspect of Carnival, perhaps not detecting the underlying edge of bitterness and resentment that accompanied the negroes' laughter.

In the distant past Carnival did occasionally witness overt violence, not so much directed against authority as exchanged between rival Carnival negro groups. It is only since the war that the aggressive side of Carnival seems to have almost completely vanished. As one observer – brought up in Trinidad before the war – put it when he returned to see Carnival again a few year ago, 'the feeling of menace has gone out of it'.

Perhaps its place has been taken by competition, which is fierce between participants. Not only is there the Band of the Year contest; there are prizes for Band Queen, calypso players, limbo dancers and song writers. But without a doubt the chief spectacle is the struggle to be best band. Saldenha and Bailey, the two great rivals of the 1960s, were probably the most talked about men in Trinidad. Strictly, there are two prizes – $1,000 for the Judge's prize, $500 to the winner of the popular ballot – but usually the same band carries off both. But that is but a small part of the winner's reward. He makes money out of his costumes; above all he wins unparalleled prestige. He is impresario, team-captain and stage-star – all in one.

Carnival is a fertile ground for invention and ingenious improvisation. Newspapers a century back wrote disparagingly of 'bands of music *(soi-disant)* including those elegant instruments the tin kettle and salt-box, the banjee and shack-shack' (the latter made of gourds with rattling pips inside); but for Carnival followers then and now, the more instruments the better. Garbage-can lids are stolen in hundreds on Shrove Monday. Biscuit-tins and paint-containers make fine percussion too. Scribo Maloney and Ellie Manette, famous pioneers of the steel band which originated through similar rough improvisation, discovered after World War II that a 44-gallon petrol drum could be tuned, and scales played on it.

Carnival has thrived on its ability to improvise, and to absorb different influences. East Indians, most of them descended from indentured laborers brought over between 1870 and 1917, and now 37% of the populace to the negroes' 43%, have added their own rituals.

With all its borrowings, its ramshackle mixture of music, escapism that recalls a harsh past, and impoverished yearnings, some Trinidad intellectuals deprecate Carnival for cultivating the island's tragic sense, for underlining the saying, from V S Naipaul's book *The Middle Passage*, 'Nothing was made in the West Indies'. Yet Carnival today is a flower of fantasy whose roots have been fed by many rich cultures – and whose fragrance is enjoyed by almost anyone lucky enough to be in Port-of-Spain on a Shrove Tuesday.

Rastafarians
Jamaica

Rastafarians wear 'dreadlocks and beards after Haile Selassie of Ethiopia – Ras Tafari before being crowned emperor in 1930.

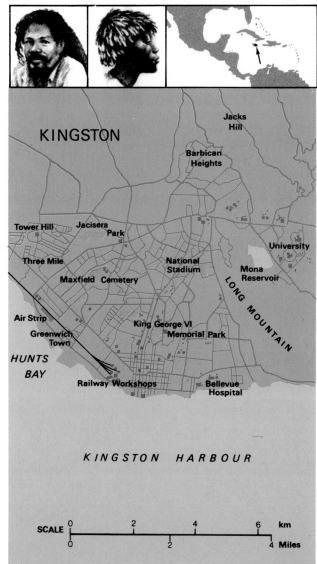

'Look to Africa when a black king shall be crowned, for deliverance is near.' These prophetic words are said to have been uttered by Marcus Garvey; and they stuck in the collective memory of his followers, until their apparent fulfillment in 1930 triggered off one of the most bizarre politico-religious cults of this century.

Garvey can be regarded as the founding father of the Rastafarian brotherhood, and also of the more recent 'Black Power' and associated movements within the United States. Born in Jamaica in 1885, he was anxious from the start to improve the condition of negroes there. He met with little success; but during World War I he went to New York and there established the Universal Negro Improvement Association, which became a mass movement of considerable influence.

He believed passionately that the black man should 35

Rastafarians live in the poorer suburbs of Kingston. Dunghill, the center of their community, is some six miles from the middle of town.

not consider himself inferior to the white man, or feel obliged to develop within white society and on white terms. His proper destiny, Garvey maintained, lay in the rediscovery of his African identity and in a return to the African homeland. Garvey went so far as to establish a special shipping line for repatriation, but this failed, and he was imprisoned simply because his ideas were uncongenial to the white master-race.

Possibly for reasons of this kind, he enjoyed only a limited political career in Jamaica after his deportation from the United States in 1927. He established the People's Political Party and secured a seat on the City Council of Kingston; but he was also jailed for contempt of court, and soon afterwards left for England. He died in 1940. An unsuccessful career by some standards; but he had initiated an enormous and still-continuing change in the consciousness, and in the sense of identity among black peoples in the New World, and he has his place in history.

In 1930, Haile Selassie – previously known as Ras

Tafari – was crowned as Emperor of Ethiopia; and at once, among the poor and unemployed black people of Jamaica, Garvey's prophecy was remembered. A black king *had* been crowned in Africa: deliverance must be at hand! It did not stop there. Among these people, so deeply religious and superstitious too, so prone to messianic and miraculous imaginings, the idea rapidly spread that Haile Selassie was actually a god who had come to earth to lead the black children of Israel home from the Babylonian captivity of white oppression.

So the Rastafarian cult began; it developed rapidly, on complex and often contradictory lines, with different schools of thought and never with anything like a formal structure. But four distinctive elements ran through all its versions from the beginning. The believer asserted the divinity of Haile Selassie; the inherent superiority of the black races; the importance of an early return to the African homeland; and finally the importance – in the meantime – of detachment from Jamaican society.

This detachment took various forms. At its simplest and most religious, it was a retreat from the world, comparable to some aspects of Catholic monasticism and some kinds of Protestant theology. Like the members of so many illuminist cults down the centuries, the Rastafarian believed he owed no allegiance to the worldly and corrupt society around him, or even to its courts of law, but only to the kingdom that was to come. These views, volubly asserted by defendants in open court, did much to foster the idea that all Rastafarians were insane. But this aspect of their movement was socially harmless: it prompted a withdrawal from Jamaican society, rather than any revolutionary desire to change it. And at their best, the Rastafarians displayed a pride and independence of spirit that one can respect, a refusal to beg or work for wages. Many of them lived by fishing and farming and various crafts; some established communes and attempted to live a common unselfish life apart, on a basis of peace and love.

Unfortunately, this kind of dedication proved neither widespread nor long-lasting, and the cult's basic posture of opposition to established Jamaican society attracted towards it many people who were anti-social on less religious lines. Some had bitterly given up hope of ever finding employment; some were rebellious teenagers from middle-class homes; some were idlers and troublemakers who would not wish to work anywhere or on any terms; and many were straightforward criminals. Before long the aggressive element became dominant, and the cult began to acquire a reputation for violence.

Today there are, perhaps, some twenty thousand people in the slums and shanty-town area of Kingston who can be called Rastafarians in one sense or another. Most of these people are concentrated on waste land on the western side of the town, an area of small and flimsy hovels, rather unfortunately known as the Dung-hill (pronounced Dungle). Above these squalid dwellings

36

Haile Selassie's portrait is proudly exhibited. He caused sharp disappointment when he came to Kingston in 1966: he looked small and semitic.

20,000 Rastafarians live in
slums and shanty towns
around Kingston, Jamaica.
Here huts are surrounded
by an automobile graveyard.

This young boy, unlike his father, is already growing his hair in the Rastafarian style, copied from Ethiopian warriors.

This young couple may never be married. Young men come and go but women regard producing and looking after children as life's role.

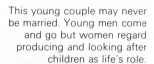

one can often see the red-and-yellow-and-green flag of Ethiopia flying bravely, and there are many notices and inscriptions, making it clear that the inhabitants think of themselves as Africans and Ethiopians, owing no allegiance at all to Jamaica. The white visitor will be advised to steer clear of them. Their reputation for violence may be exaggerated, but they do not welcome strangers.

Even in this land of eccentricity, the Rastafarian – if and when you meet him – will present a remarkably bizarre appearance. He will wear rags, sometimes colorful and sometimes merely drab, and a long disheveled beard following the example of the distant bearded Emperor; his hair will be arranged in dread-locks which earn their name, since they have often put terror into the hearts of respectable Jamaicans. It is an eccentric hair-style, copied from pictures of Ethiopian warriors: the long hair is twisted into spiky vertical strands, and it is said that the adhesive used to keep it in place is sometimes animal-dung.

In these Kingston slums, where a wrecked car offers palatial accommodation, the Rastafarians lead a chiefly nocturnal and remarkably empty life. They feed themselves largely by fishing; they spend a great deal of their time in political discussion, in reverential thoughts

of the Emperor, and in dreaming of their African future. But here life's great occupation and comfort is smoking *ganja,* the local name for marijuana. Rastafarians believe they have biblical authority for regarding this 'wisdom weed' as a sacred thing, prescribed by God, in Genesis, spiritually uniting the smoker to Him, and conferring health, wisdom, and strength; and their ultimate anger is reserved for any individual or organization which presumes to separate them from the *ganja.* Unfortunately the Jamaican government is a case in point, since the drug is illegal there as in many other countries: it is for this reason, and not on account of violence, that almost every Rastafarian has a police and prison record.

Between them and the public authorities, there has for long existed a state of continued smouldering hostility, especially since about 1955, when the country communes broke up and the dreadlocks moved into Kingston in force. From then on, the Rastafarians became increasingly disliked by the community at large; many leaders were arrested on charges of sedition or disorderly conduct, and anyone who adhered to the movement – or even dressed or wore his hair in the Rastafarian style – was likely to find himself harrassed and victimized by employers, landlords, police and courts. Even wearing a beard can lead to a beating-up, and the Rastafarian, no matter how innocent, does not easily find a defender when in trouble.

They are a pathetic people, deeply bemused by drugs and propaganda, hooked upon their visionary hope, and only tenuously in touch with any kind of reality. Their health appears remarkably good – though probably not because of the *ganja* to which they would give the credit. But their mental level is low, and actual insanity is common among them: at the best, they tend to be impervious to any kind of reasoned argument about the subject matter of their faith. It is no use telling a dedicated believer that his own origins are West African, and that the Emperor and people of Ethiopia belong to a different and chiefly semitic race; it is no good reminding him that British troops liberated Ethiopia from Italian occupation during the World War II, and might deserve some credit for this. He will sweep all such ideas aside, as exemplifying the untruthful propaganda of the white man's history books. He prefers to believe the wise men of his own people; and they will tell him, consistently and with total assurance, that he is an Ethiopian by race, and that no white man (with the possible exception of the Russians) has ever done any good thing.

This quasi-Zionist faith of the Rastafarians, in the imminence of their own return to Africa, might seem as unrealistic as the hopes of those who follow Cargo Cults in New Guinea and Melanesia. But they are not entirely unrealistic. There is, after all, the historical precedent of Liberia; and in 1955 Haile Selassie actually allocated

Even young children smoke 'grass' wrapped in banana leaves – for it is life's great compensation among unrealized dreams of Africa.

a proportion of Ethiopian land for the occupation of black peoples who might decide to immigrate from the New World. The news of this – coming at a time when emigration was in the air already, by reason of the steady flow of Jamaicans to England – caused great excitement at Kingston; and three years later, about three thousand Rastafarians assembled in a kind of convention, which lasted for 21 riotous days, inspired by a belief that the return to Africa was imminent. The fires, dancings and tumult of those three weeks confirmed the prevailing belief that Rastafarians were insane and dangerously misguided. Shortly afterwards, in 1960, passions were further inflamed by the nearest thing possible to a Rastafarian revolution.

It was a small and hopeless affair. A man called Claudius Henry set up as a prophetic leader and announced that he would lead his followers back to Africa on a specified date, provided that each of them paid him ten cents for the ticket. From his own point of view, this intelligent scheme succeeded perfectly: fifteen thousand of them paid up – some of them even disposed of the Jamaican possessions that they would need no more – and Henry was richer by some $1,500.

The specified date came and went, and he had to devise a series of plausible explanations for the unexpected delay. Soon suspicions were aroused, there was a police raid on his headquarters, and a modest cache of arms was discovered, together with two letters addressed to Fidel Castro asking for his help in the conquest of Jamaica. Henry was arrested and imprisoned for treason. Soon afterwards his son arrived in Jamaica and took to the hills with a band of guerrillas, apparently with a view to a *coup d'état*: his father's unkind confidence trick was presumably intended to finance the operation. At all events, the younger Henry was soon captured; but not before there had been some fighting, in the course of which two British soldiers and three Rastafarians were killed. The threat to the Jamaican government had not been serious; but the fact of bloodshed aroused strong feelings, and public hostility to the cult became fiercer.

In this situation, certain more sober minds felt that an objectively factual study of the Rastafarians' way of life and aspirations might help to improve relations. An academic team from what was then the University College of the West Indies was briefed to undertake this study; and they soon reported that only a few of the Rastafarians were the criminal lunatics of popular belief. The great majority, they said, were in the normal condition of the unemployed and underprivileged, and deserved to be pitied and helped rather than despised and avoided. The prevailing attitude could do nothing but harm. If these people continued to be treated on lines only appropriate to an extremist minority among them, this could only foster their slight but real tendency towards Marxist or racial revolution. Finally, the report

With his pipe full of 'grass' this Rastafarian has formed his 'dreadlocks' with animal dung. His fantasies can erupt into violence.

(Bottom) A couple prepare a simple meal in their shack. Most live in the waste land known as Dunghill but pronounced 'Dungle'.

took seriously the Rastafarians' desire to return to Africa, and recommended that practical steps should be taken to make this possible.

This report was greeted with stupefaction and then with strongly-worded objection: many people, black and white, made it clear that they looked upon the Rastafarians as drug-sodden, good-for-nothing hooligans, upon whom any kind of gentleness or consideration would be wasted. It was also asserted that no African state would want them.

But the Jamaican government took the commission's

Fishing involves no
participation in Jamaican
society. Hence it is one
of the most popular
Rastafarian activities.

advice, and in 1961 a semi-official mission – including three Rastafarians – actually set off for Africa to look into the possibilities of immigration. They visited Ethiopia, Liberia, Sierra Leone, Ghana and Nigeria, and in each of these countries the principle of repatriation was accepted, though with various reservations about the type of people who would be likely to come. Haile Selassie was particularly enthusiastic and friendly.

The dreamer's psychology, however, is complicated: he would prefer to retain the familiar and cherished dream, rather than to suffer the uncertainties of its sudden fulfillment. And now, as that long-cherished hope of a return to Africa began to show signs of actually coming to pass, many of the Rastafarians began to have second thoughts. Soon a program of the opposite kind was attracting attention in black Jamaica generally: this was led by Millard Johnson in the spirit of Marcus Garvey. The proposal was that instead of black Jamaicans returning to Africa, they should devote themselves to the radical Africanization of Jamaica.

This much less unsettling plan was greeted with something like a collective sigh of relief by the Rastafarian community which reverted once more to dreams of Ethiopia. Those plans for emigration came to nothing. But the whole episode, from the academic commission's report onwards, did something to foster a more humane and tolerant attitude towards people whose crazy religion and reputation for violence were attributable – in the last resort – to their poverty. Meanwhile the Rastafarians, who have added fame to notoriety as principal originators of the now international reggae music, show no signs of calming down. A recent reggae hit promised 'Blood, blood, blood, blood and fire.'

They may stand in need of comfort, since the faith by which they live has recently sustained a shock. In 1966 the Emperor Haile Selassie visited Jamaica. He was greeted at the airport by an enormous crowd of ecstatic Rastafarians. During his stay some were temporarily recognized by the Government and elevated above their usual outcast status to participate in the official celebrations. It was their great day: it was, after all, their god who was visiting the country.

But gods should not come too close to the earth. The Emperor turned out to be a disappointingly small man; his features were clearly more semitic than negroid; and he had arrived by air, in the style of a common millionaire rather than a god.

The Rastafarians were disillusioned. But the right kind of faith can overcome all difficulties; and the doubters soon managed to convince themselves that yet another white man's trick had been played, and that the so-called 'Emperor' was in fact an impostor. 41

The Last of the Caribs
Dominica

Dominica was too rainy to
attract many British planters.
Almost everyone has land and
the island is more content
than its neighbors.

The largest remnant of the race that once dominated the Caribbean is found today on Dominica, an island 29 miles long and 16 miles across, almost in the center of a chain of islands known as the Lesser Antilles. Christopher Columbus discovered Dominica on Sunday 3 November 1493, and so it acquired its name. The Dominican Republic, part of the much larger island of Hispaniola further north, has the same name and the two places are forever being confused. At that time the island was occupied by Caribs, a warlike people who fiercely resisted European attempts to settle on their island. For over a century they were successful, until the French began to establish settlements and brought in numbers of slaves from Africa. The British intervened and there was continuous fighting for most of the next century and a half, until the island was eventually ceded to Britain in 1763. The slaves were emancipated in 1834.

43

Columbus came in 1493. The French came next, then the British. You often hear a compound *patois* in Roseau, the sea-girt capital.

In 1967 the island became virtually independent as an associated state.

Dominica is the last home in the eastern Caribbean of the Caribs, the region's early inhabitants. The Caribs who lived in other islands of the lesser Antilles were killed in the wars with Europeans, succumbed to disease, or were shipped off to British Honduras, where they intermarried with the negroes and therefore came to be called 'Black Caribs'; the Caribs on Dominica on the other hand, remained aloof from their negro neighbors, and although some have intermarried, a few hundred relatively pure-blooded Caribs still live on the small Carib reservation at Salybia on the rocky, windswept windward coast. They still have the marked Mongolian features, high cheekbones, slit eyes and smooth black hair – the envy of all the negroes – that so astounded Columbus and his men. They were convinced that the Caribs must have come down from the north. In fact they had . . . but long centuries before: they entered the Caribbean not from the north but from the Amazon basin, whence they had made their way northwards from island to island, killing and eating the peaceful Arawaks they found living there. They were cannibals, the first any European had yet encountered. Columbus was horrified by the sight of barbecued human limbs hanging from the roof timbers of Carib houses. He wrote home about the disgusting habits of the 'Caribals' – the people

In a convent in Roseau Dominica's women go to work flexible hours at crafts once practised by African ancestors.

Once subsistence farmers,
most of the country people
now grow cash crops. Like
this woman, they sell their
goods in the market.

of the Caribee islands – and so the word 'cannibal' came into use.

Now five centuries later, only this tiny community of a few hundred Caribs still survives. They have long since ceased to be cannibals, and today they are peaceful farmers and Roman Catholics. They differ from their negro neighbors only in their distinctive features, and in small details of their nature and their way of life; a love of flowers round their huts, a passion for rum exceeding even that of the negro, their age-old skill at making and sailing canoes, their tradition of basket-making, and the fact that they still have their own chief with his sash of office. Their ancient languages (they had no less than three) have vanished, although a few vestiges still remain in English – for example 'hammock', 'hurricane' and 'canoe'.

The Caribs of Dominica were for years a forgotten people. They could no longer fight, they would not be slaves, and they despised the negroes for submitting to white masters. They had no friends, the negroes regarding them as an inferior people, whilst the slave-owners feared that by their example they might encourage marooning – running away into the woods to escape slavery. They were treated like gypsies, ignored if possible or regarded simply as a nuisance. So they lapsed into obscurity and poverty. Until quite recent times they had no school, no shops, no doctors, no church and until 1903, when the reservation was established, no legal right to the land they occupied.

Today the Caribs are enjoying the minor boom that has come to Dominica since World War II. They have become banana growers. They now have a beautiful church and a devoted priest, and a flourishing school. Education in this school has a distinctively British flavor. Children's exercise books include such sentences as: 'In the winter we make snowmen.' It never snows in Dominica.

The future of this little community lies with these bright-eyed youngsters, a truly new generation of Caribs. Their education will bring them closer to the mainstream of Dominican society; they will surely want to become full Dominicans rather than a race apart to be visited by the tourist like a rare species of animal. In time they will probably become indistinguishable from other Dominicans. For the moment however, this little community of Caribs survives as a recognizable ethnic group, the last remnant of a once powerful people who made their way from Asia across the Bering Strait, through Alaska, north and central America and the Amazon jungle, who became formidable seamen, building war canoes each capable of carrying 100 men, and who first conquered the Caribbean islands.

Apart from the Caribs and a few hundred people of European and other nationalities, the seventy thousand inhabitants of Dominica are negroes, descendants of slaves brought over from Africa. Some of them are pure 45

46

Dominica's Caribs, like this
dreamy-eyed woman, are now
almost the only survivors
of the Indian race that once
populated all the islands.

black, but the majority are of mixed blood. Their ancestors came from the Guinea coast in the dark, stinking holds of the slave ships. Many survived only to die in hundreds in the hot rainforests of Dominica, chopping down the huge gommier trees and planting coffee and sugar. The interior of Dominica is one of the wettest places on the globe – in places, as much as 400 inches of rain falls in a year. The mortality rate among slaves was particularly high in Dominica, due probably to these terrible conditions.

In Dominica, when emancipation came, the slaves were not embittered; despite all the hardships and indignities they had undergone, they did not, as one might expect, develop an irreparable sense of grievance. Nor do they have one now. The reason is probably that sugar was never king on Dominica, and the plantation system never became firmly established. The conditions were too bad, the endless wars with the French and the maroons inhibited development, and the principal crops failed one after the other; first coffee, then sugar and cocoa. Many estates owned by white people became bankrupt and were sold to the peasants after emancipation, so that Dominica became a peasant-farmer community. Nearly everyone owned some land and grew his own food. The Dominican was poor, but he would not starve, and he had a stake in the land. The typical Dominican has always had close links with the soil, and with it the countryman's shrewdness and wisdom. Dominica has never known a large landless class of laborers since emancipation, and this has given her remarkable internal stability. Until very recently the island was a by-word in the Caribbean for the contentedness of its inhabitants in a part of the world that has been passing through some cataclysmic changes.

In common with most of the Caribbean peoples, the typical Dominican has a happy attitude to life, he laughs easily and is generally tolerant by nature. More than most Caribbean people, the Dominican has a relatively unsophisticated philosophy of life, as yet little affected by urban values. There are no large towns, and his pleasures are mostly simple ones. He enjoys playing or watching cricket (every village has its cricket pitch, no matter how hilly), gossiping over a drink and a game of dominoes in the bar, going to agricultural shows or choosing the latest beauty queen. The cinema is also very popular, there being no television on the island. Perhaps the Carnival best epitomizes the Dominican's love of festive occasions and this is one pleasure he really works hard at. Some say that the Dominicans are indolent – Dominicans even say it of themselves – but if they are less inclined to enter the rat-race than westerners this may be because nature has been so kind to them.

In many Dominican families it is the mother who is the central figure not the father. The institution of marriage does not occupy the same position as it does in Europe. 47

This woman fetching water is one of about 200 Caribs. Said to have eaten defeated Arawaks who were here before, they are now placid farmers.

The Carib chief stands with his mother, proudly wearing his sash of office. He was democratically elected by the tribe.

The chief of the island's Caribs stands with his deputy leader before his tribe's church. Caribs are now devout Catholics.

According to legend, his ancestors paddled across from the central American mainland in 100 canoes. Today's remnant clings to its language.

It is still as much respected but as little practised as it has ever been. Only about a third of Dominican couples get married. This may be due to many factors, but, ironically, one of the most important is the cost of the marriage ceremony itself. Women are willing to co-habit and produce children without the security of the marriage ceremony, and many of these relationships are lasting and happy – they are called 'faithful concubinage' or 'common law marriage.' Society also tends to associate proven virility with manhood; to have fathered a bastard child is no shame for the father, and if a woman has not proved her fertility by the age of 20, she risks being called a 'mule.' As a result, the rate of population growth in Dominica is very high, one of the highest in the Caribbean, and over half the population is under 20. Although successful family groupings are often established without the ceremony of marriage, there are nevertheless too many children running about the streets of the towns and villages lacking the companionship and correction of a father – and often the continuous love and care of a mother, who may have to work to maintain the family. The clergy of all denominations have striven for centuries to institute marriage as the norm rather than the exception: their lack of success in such a religious society as Dominica is a remarkable indication of the strength of long-established attitudes.

Roman Catholicism is by far the most dominant religion in Dominica; about 90 per cent of the population are Catholic. Most of the priests are French, and *patois* is still the language of the majority of the people, although about 60 per cent can now speak English, the official language. As *patois* is not a written language there is no indigenous literature or poetry. In the villages the stone churches are usually the only substantial buildings among the small wooden huts of the peasants – except perhaps the government school – and the priests have always occupied a key role in community life. On Sunday mornings, to go to church, the people dress in their best clothes, which they keep especially washed and ironed for this weekly airing, their children wearing their neatest plaits and broadest smiles. Religious parades are held to celebrate the main church festivals, and these add a colorful dimension to life in Roseau – the principal town – and in the larger villages.

In recent years, with the spread of education and public services, and the growing urbanization centered on Roseau (now about 18,000 people), the church has tended to lose its dominant position in society. People are becoming increasingly mobile, and less 'parochial' in their interests. Even the Caribs travel more frequently into Roseau to do their shopping and to spend the money they earn growing bananas. New roads are opening up areas that until recently were so remote that mail took a week to arrive from Roseau, and a doctor or midwife took a day, no matter how urgent the summons. Now the great majority of children go to school (although still too many can be seen head-loading bananas for their parents when they should be learning), and an increasing proportion attend grammar school. The church is also moving with the times and has introduced a Caribbean version of the Mass complete with local music. Underlying all these changes is the great economic development that has taken place in Dominica during the last 20 years since the banana industry began to expand after World War II. At that time the peasants grew *cassava* – a root vegetable pounded into flour – and vegetables, mostly for their own consumption. Then along came Geests with a long-term contract for bananas, and soon everyone seemed to be growing bananas. So much so that some peasants have ceased to grow their own food and prefer to buy what they require in the shops. The Dominicans have now become accustomed to a money economy when only a generation ago theirs was a mainly subsistence economy. As yet this has not produced many obvious changes in the rural areas, although there have been remarkable developments in Roseau, where many public buildings have gone up in the last ten years and where major re-housing schemes have been carried out. The peasants have been slow to show their increased prosperity from bananas in such ways as improving their houses or buying furniture, although their expenditure on rum and tobacco has risen.

Dominican society since the beginning of the 1970s has come under pressure from two directions. First, there are signs of a Black Power movement led by the teenage boys who have adopted the 'Afro' hairstyle. From street corners they shout 'honky' at the tourists and white visitors, but early in 1972 a more serious incident occurred. Some boys wearing this hairstyle were sent home from St Mary's Academy to have their hair groomed. They interpreted this as an act of racialism and instigated a protest march to the Prime Minister who gave them a sympathetic hearing. As a result the school was closed and the Christian Brothers, who had supplied the teaching staff, left Dominica.

The second source of tension is the growing rift between town and country. The capital, Roseau, has become dominated by the opposition Freedom Party, whilst the government Labour Party represents more the traditional rural interest. In 1971 and 1972 several thousand people took part in political protest marches. The townsman enjoys comparative affluence in contrast to the peasant in the villages who still lives in his two-roomed wooden shack with probably no running water and a latrine out in the yard. If the tourist industry begins to flourish, as seems likely, there will be conspicuous affluence in the midst of poverty, and experience elsewhere in the Caribbean has shown that this is a sure recipe for internal unrest and tension. The period of internal stability and contentedness that has characterized Dominican society since mid-century may be yielding to a more unsettled period.

49

Caribbean
Tourist's playground

Every year nearly 5 million
tourists, almost all white,
outnumber the Caribbean
populace of 3 million — who
are almost all black.

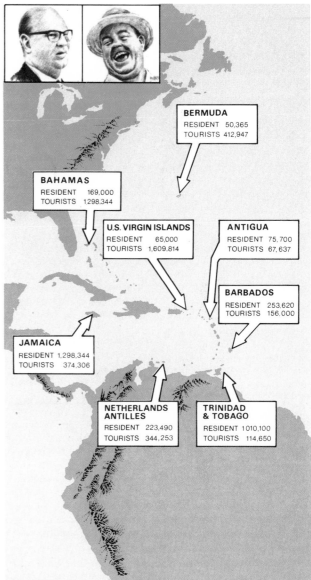

BERMUDA	
RESIDENT	50,365
TOURISTS	412,947

BAHAMAS	
RESIDENT	169,000
TOURISTS	1,298,344

U.S. VIRGIN ISLANDS	
RESIDENT	65,000
TOURISTS	1,609,814

ANTIGUA	
RESIDENT	75,700
TOURISTS	67,637

BARBADOS	
RESIDENT	253,620
TOURISTS	156,000

JAMAICA	
RESIDENT	1,298,344
TOURISTS	374,306

NETHERLANDS ANTILLES	
RESIDENT	223,490
TOURISTS	344,253

TRINIDAD & TOBAGO	
RESIDENT	1,010,100
TOURISTS	114,650

Every year nearly four and a half million tourists, almost all white, swarm into the Caribbean, whose resident population of just over three million is almost all black. Most of the white tourists are Americans; virtually all the black Caribbeans are negroes. Most of the Caribbean depends economically on tourism and, in places, also on retired white residents from the US. The United States itself takes the situation for granted – even encourages it when it has an economic or political responsibility – as in Puerto Rico or the American Virgin Islands. This is how the US Department of the Interior pamphlet describes the Virgins:

These storybook islands have a magical charm – in the beat of steel drums, in a language with a Calypso lilt, in 51

(Top) To its glorified
holiday-camp and ever-blue
sky, the port of Nassau, the
Bahamas' capital, greets
tourists (and tax-evaders).

In the sweltering heat,
a police constable stands
on duty emulating his
London counterpart in
both dress and dignity.

their history, in their architecture. *Seven flags have flown
over the Virgin Islands – the Dutch, the Danish, the
French, the Knights of Malta, the Spanish, the British,
and the United States – and their influences are woven
into a distinctive cultural pattern to be found nowhere else
in the world. From the sun-drenched beaches to the
numerous misty mountain peaks, a visit to the Virgin
Islands is an adventure one will never forget.*

The notable exception is Cuba. The most famous
restaurant in Havana serves today only very basic meals.
Once, in Batista's day, before the Revolution, and the
resulting US boycott, it .was different. But the restaurant still keeps its visitors' book. Erroll Flynn is one
of the many famous signatures. Beside his name he
scrawled cheerfully: 'the best place to get drunk.' So it
was, then. Indeed, all Havana was: a mildly orgiastic
playground for the people of the eastern American
seaboard. In poured the Americans, to the vast air-
conditioned towers, where they drank and wenched, and
toasted themselves on the rims of swimming pools fifty
feet from the sea itself. In those days – the 1950s – Cuba
enjoyed the highest living standards in Latin America.
Since then their standard of living has been halved.
Cubans have not seen an American tourist since 1960.

They have paid the economic penalty. Their reward, they
say, is their *dignidad.*

Tourism and *dignidad,* self-respect, do not easily go
together. Tourism on a massive scale amid small and
vulnerable communities makes the traditional life of the
community self-conscious; it commercializes and cor-
rupts both outwardly and intimately.

The utopian image of the Virgins in the US Department of the Interior's pamphlet is belied by the realities.
The islanders know that the continuing tourist boom has
become economically essential. They must doggedly
sustain the holiday enthusiasm year in year out. (Sometimes as many as five cruise ships at a time anchor off
Puerto Rico to disgorge two or three thousand passengers
into Charlotte Amalie's crowded streets.) Virgin Islanders and Puerto Ricans have had to put up with an influx
of some twenty thousand 'alien' black immigrants (out
of a total of some sixty-five thousand) from the British,
French and Dutch West Indies, who have been imported
to fill the jobs created by the 'paradise boom'. Workers
have flocked to St Thomas and St Croix from Antigua,
St Kitts, Anguilla, Nevis and even from as far as
Trinidad. Nearly half the work force is now comprised
of 'bonded aliens', as they are known, from 'down

(Bottom) The decorum of an
English county court was long
ago brought to the Bahamas,
where British colonial
tradition is proudly upheld.

island'. Much of the need for new labor is to build the homes and chalets of expatriate Americans.

The late President Kennedy of the US spoke of the American Virgins becoming a 'showcase of democracy'. The boom brought about by the islands' natural attractions of climate and beauty, and artificial attractions of tax advantages, has meant that the power has gone not to the indigenous people of the islands, but to the interloper and – indirectly – to the visitor. The roads leading out of the towns are flanked by swarms of shacks. Rambling settlements of shacks in the towns themselves contrast vividly with the duty-free shops, filled with luxuries, and with the fine hotels and villas along the coastline.

The pattern is repeated in varying forms throughout most of the Caribbean, although most other islands have been endeavoring to export their populations rather than import others. Barbados, for example, draws a significant proportion of its tourists and sun-seeking immigrants from Britain. It retains a British style in its holiday package. A placid and beautiful isle, its mainly negro population has come to be thought too deferential towards its whites by its more turbulent and ambitious Caribbean neighbors. Expanding US investment and tourism imply an impending change.

In Jamaica, where tourism has been built up as a major industry from the early 1950s, the very success of the trade is now recognized as a problem. North American tourists outnumber other tourists by 50 to 1. Virtually all the 374,000 holiday-makers coming into Jamaica go to the north coast, which has become an all-American playground. The food in the tourist hotels is American – even the spelling and style of the menus is Americanized: waiters and staff of the hotels adopt American accents. The non-American soon learns to tip on the American scale (never less than 15 per cent), or his holiday becomes a succession of sullen glances and service becomes reluctant. The hotel staff make a mild mockery of their own traditions for the sake of their visitors, and you can find waiters dancing in with trays of drinks on their heads and porters wearing topees, scarlet monkey jackets, purple cummerbunds, white cotton shorts and scarlet socks.

Communal entertainment is laid on in an American style. Hotels are designed to prevent the need to set foot beyond their boundaries, and the guest lives in a kind of glorified holiday camp; a military base, as it were, on permanent leave in what might or might not be a hostile country. In plush hotels in Ocho Rios and Montego Bay, tourists in their thousands are playing bingo, taking part in crab racing, doing competitive dancing in funny hats. The night before they leave they find 'come again' written in scarlet cats' tails (a kind of tropical pussy willow) on their tables.

They cha-cha-cha after dinner in Bermuda shorts, take part in guest fashion shows, and as a forfeit in a statue dance they find themselves joining a group of other couples in which the husbands, dressed as babies in bibs and bonnets, sit on their wives' knees to be suckled on fruit juice from babies' bottles (photographs of such hilarities available in the foyer next morning at $2 each). Negro minstrel teams entertain diners with calypsos including the famous *Workin' for the Yankee dollar* (with a verse about the rising financial expectation of the local playgirls).

Official government exhortations on the virtues of looking after the tourists attempt to restore the balance of self respect. Posters on display and tourist centers – Montego Bay, Ocho Rios, Port Antonio, Kingston – instruct the people on 'what we must do to keep the tourists coming in increasing numbers.' For instance: 'From the moment the visitors arrive, let us make them feel welcome. . . . This attitude is necessary on the part of us all, not just those engaged in the tourist industry. . . . Let us make Jamaican service second to none in the world, and let us not confuse good service with servility. Let us all make the visitors aware that we Jamaicans are proud of our country. Tell them of our progress socially, politically and economically. Let us not cry down our island to visitors. Show visitors how Jamaicans live. Let us encourage them to take part in our community activities.'

It is not easy to realize these reasonable sentiments. The black-skinned Jamaican peasant, scratching a living from the cocoa, yams, maize, bananas and okra (ladies' fingers) from his steep little patch cannot wait beside the road to show the tourists how he lives. The unemployed thousands (probably as much as 20 per cent of the whole population) in their grim slum hovels of mud, board and tin do not find it easy to 'make the visitors aware that we Jamaicans are proud of our country.'

What does 'Workin' for the Yankee dollar' mean for those not in the tourist industry? To a group of school boys, stopped by a tourist in St James' Street, Montego Bay, one noon tide, it might mean doing the Rock for him in the street, the best one receiving a Yankee dollar. To countless other children in all the towns where tourists go it means unashamed begging and badgering as the visitors meander from shop to restaurant. It means catering for the more intimate appetites of visiting ladies, among the tourists, whose white civilization makes them somehow unsatisfied.

Jamaica is calling, the travel brochure croons, *to all the work-weary and routine-drugged who long for a little reprieve. Jamaica – that 'tropical island' you have been dreaming of – an island rich in history of pirates and buccaneers, as quaint as native huts tucked away behind tropical foliage, as modern as today's luxury hotels. Rugged, lofty mountains bumping the puffy white clouds that drift across the postcard-blue skies. Magical nights of dancing under the stars, and always the tinkling silver moonlight path across the water to the moon.*

The immediate effect on indigenous islanders of the 53

tourist surge is one of excitement at the expanded economic opportunities. Peasant life can be set aside for jobs in construction, the hotel trade and even – for the talented – show business: steel band performers (in Trinidad and Tobago), calypso singers, limbo performers, and so on. The local handicraft trade in straw hats and dolls and the like swells too.

Yet soon enough the continued thrusting up of a basically poor and backward tropical community against an unending invasion of better-off white citizens from the dominant northern culture begins to tell. Caribbean society, capriciously seeded from slaves and settlers, is anyway inherently unstable. Black power manifestations in Trinidad, Rastafarians in Jamaica, symptoms of political extremism in Bermuda and the Bahamas, the Dutch Antilles (Curaçao, Bonaire and Aruba) and Haiti, tell the same story. The compound of envy, frustration and self-disgust, which the role as a tourist playground helps to create, is a new source of volatility in much of the Caribbean.

Any visitor to Trinidad
Can have good time he never had
If he come just for rest, okay
Then he lie around in sun all day.

Drinkin' Rum and Coca Cola
Go down 'Point Koomahnah'
Both mother and daughter
Workin' for the Yankee dollar.

In every Isle on Caribbean Sea
Native girl dress peculiarly
She wear Sarong, like native should
But Sarong is only dish-towel that 'make good'.

Drinkin' Rum and Coca Cola . . .

In Botanical Gardens in afternoons
Native bands play Yankee tunes
Native dance until he drop
I think Native blow his top.

Drinkin' Rum and Coca Cola . . .

Native girl can cut a rug
Dance like crazy Jitterbug
She jump and bump and shake so bold
That's fine way to break up a cold.

Drinkin' Rum and Coca Cola . . .

In Tuna-puna, it is said,
Native carry everything on her head.
This so hard on head, I hear . . .
She use fifty ton of Aspirin each year.

Drinkin' Rum and Coca Cola . . .

I bought a dog in Trinidad,
Best darn dog I ever had.
He so smart that little pup
Walk on front legs . . . if you hold back ones up.

Drinkin' Rum and Coca Cola . . .

When soldier go parading by
Native girls all wink the eye
Help soldier celebrate his leave
Make every day like New Year's Eve.

Drinkin' Rum and Coca Cola . . .

A retired British navy commander, now a thriving restaurateur, adds to the holiday mood of his hotel by dressing up in a grass skirt.

54

US businessmen in baby caps
round off a jolly two weeks
in Jamaica. Next day they can
buy photos of themselves
in the hotel foyer.

Voodoo cultists
Haiti

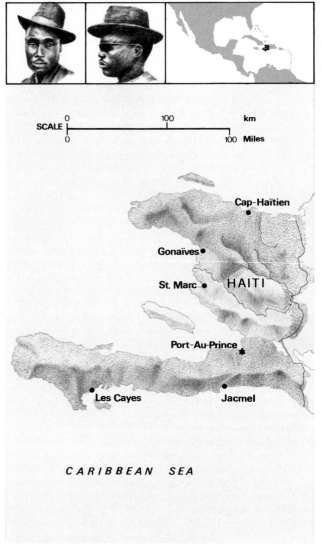

Among the cluttered streets and hillside shanties, the government offices and ministerial residences of the oldest negro republic in the world, there exists a dimension of secret awe peculiar to that community. The evil eye is at work.

The island of Sainte-Domingue, of which today's Haiti is the western third, was France's richest colony. But in 1791 the island underwent a remarkable and brilliant revolution that shocked even the Jacobins of France. It was captured and successfully defended by rebel black slaves under Toussaint L'Ouverture, who was later tricked by French negotiators and died a prisoner in the Château de Joux in the Jura mountains. Since then, the history of Haiti (split from its neighbor, the Dominican Republic, in the 1840s) has been scarred by violence and racial hatred.

Haiti's raison d'être is its blackness. Despite this fact,

57

In the center of this voodoo
altar sits the late dictator
Papa Doc Duvalier. In
Haiti, voodoo and political
tyranny run together.

Haiti, the poorest country
in the Americas, comes last
in the league in expectation
of life (44·5 years), average
income and adult literacy.

58

Throbbing drums, a legacy
of Haitians' African
origins, resound with
intricately woven rhythms to
announce a voodoo ceremony.

Religious fervor glazes
the eyes of a singing and
entranced devotee, as she
falls under the spell
of spirits and drums.

the mulattos who make up ten per cent of the five million population are the élite. Their most famous member in recent years was François Duvalier, known to his subjects and the world as Papa Doc. 'President for life', he died in 1971 after a reign of terror that lasted 14 years. Chubby 20-year-old 'Baby Doc' followed his father as president. Where power really lies is not always entirely certain.

It was Duvalier Père who created the infamous Ton Ton Macoutes, *a handpicked police force trained in the exercise of terror primarily in defence of the president. In the capital of Port-au-Prince they may be seen swaggering through the streets, gun on hip, dark glasses half hiding their faces. Papa Doc told them 'You are black, you are ugly, you smell – but you have power'. They are above the law and the Haitians fear their brutality. Many are voodoo priests. Not only do they monopolize power; they also rake in for themselves and the leaders much of the nation's wealth.*

Average income in Haiti is $70 a year and life expectancy is below 40. But the mountainous countryside is beautiful and fertile and potentially one of the richest in the Caribbean. Reform could certainly eradicate poverty, but nearly two centuries of capricious tyranny has deadened respect for justice. Change is slight when it comes and stems only from mysterious intrigues among the élite. Even the balm of Catholicism can do little to ease the plight of Haitians. One may wonder how they suffer their lot so placidly.

The answer is voodoo. Haitians are strongly bound to their African heritage: their creole language is a hotchpotch of French and West African tongues. From African origins, Haiti has evolved in voodoo a cult that assists tyrants to rule through fear, but nonetheless gives the people's lives some meaning. The image of Papa Doc himself graces many a voodoo shrine.

A voodoo priestess, carried
away by the emotion she
feels for her god,
whips up the crowd
to share her euphoria.

Voodoo comes from the African Fon word *vodun* (or *vudowo* in Ewe). In Africa its meaning embraces the notion of god, spirit and sacred object. In Haiti it describes the beliefs and practices found in the islands whose inhabitants are mostly descendants of slaves brought over from Africa – a complex religion of many strains: black magic and superstition; benign ancestral spirits that may be asked to solve problems and help the household; gods that possess their worshippers.

Every child is brought up to fear all kinds of supernatural beings; fearsome wandering spirits, monsters, the midday sun, the evening dew and the *loupgarous,* the witches who suck children's blood and may sometimes be seen whizzing through the night like fireworks. In fear of these formidable forces the Haitian child learns good manners. Whenever a child becomes fretful or suffers convulsions his mother will immediately suspect foul play: some jealous neighbor or malicious relative has invoked a *loupgarou* who is attacking her child. Her only remedy is to consult the magician. She begs him to discover the identity of her child's tormentor, to remove the evil from him and turn it back upon the witch who sent it. Along with his spells and incantations the magician administers to the child a magic potion – sometimes castor oil – which helps to get rid of the child's worms – and the convulsions cease. The child gets better, the witch confesses, and the poisonous atmosphere, *mauvais air* – clears. The child is relieved by the treatment of his body, and the mother by the treatment of his soul.

Magic affects the soul of either the victim or his persecutor. The soul is called the *gros bon ange* – the great good angel – and is manifested in breath and in shadow. The *ti bon ange* – the little good angel – is equated with twilight, the spirit and the conscience and is also sometimes called the *zombi*. Both angels inhabit the *corps cadavre*, or corpse body. The weak element in this trilogy is the soul, the *gros bon ange*, although without it the other two would lose contact with each other; the conscience, which is part of the *ti bon ange* – would lose touch with the body – often with drastic results. The weak element, the *gros bon ange* or soul, is easily infected by emotions like suspicion, resentment, anger, envy, greed and lust; it is easily overwhelmed by sudden shocks like a death in the family, a business failure, or a betrayal.

If he is to be cured he must become his own magician. Out of his ravings a vision may emerge, his malady personified as a spirit. He begins to decipher its messages, and as well as learning how to heal his soul, he sets up a contact with the spirit world, which outlasts his illness. Initiated in voodoo, he now starts up as a small-time priest, himself diagnosing and treating illness, giving advice and practising black and white magic for a fee.

The case histories of these minor voodooists show that trivial incidents can suddenly let loose emotions of anxiety and foreboding that have long been repressed. A man may smoke a cigarette given him by a neighbor **59**

Pain from the heat of
torch-flames keeps a
priestess semi-conscious.
Lay voodooists may collapse
but priests must dance on.

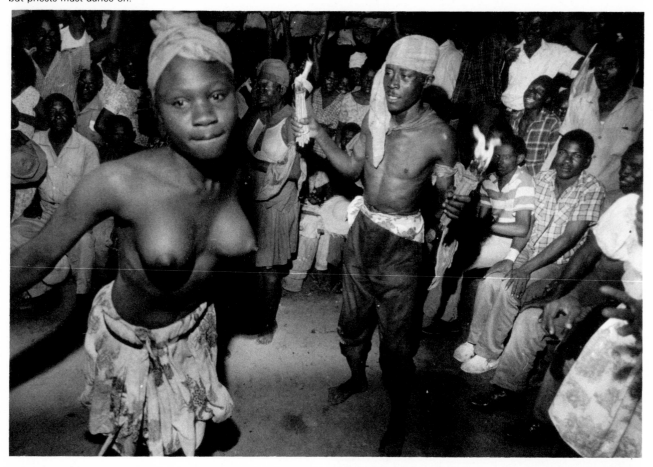

whom he has long mistrusted, and given with a meaning-
ful glance; he goes off in agitation, becomes hysterical
and then vomits up such interesting emblems of his dis-
comfiture as lizards, pieces of bark, or a large and poisonous centipede. The vomiting brings him back to himself
after what amounts to a possession. He puts what he has
vomited into a bottle and tops it up with rum. It becomes
his guardian spirit and oracle, and he uses the liquor as a
medicine for others. What has happened is that one part
of the illness – the physical poison – has been taken out
of the body and given another home (known as a
reposoire); while the other part of the illness – frustrated
emotion – becomes a controllable spirit.

The first priority of a voodoo novice is to find out
which of the spirits is afflicting him: sometimes he seeks
the help of an established voodoo priest to interpret his
saisissement or the series of calamities that besets him.
The answer is perhaps that he is being persecuted by his
neighbor for some real or imagined offence. Or it may
be that he has neglected his duties to his dead parents.
Their spirits may be calling to him from the waters of
penitence, impatient to be removed to the comfort of the
govis (pots) at the family altar, where they should
properly reside. Or maybe the gods – the *loa* or Invisibles

The movements of voodoo
dancers are spontaneous.
Possessed devotees dance
either on their own or
with fellow voodooists.

Madame Adolphe, chief of the dreaded Ton Ton Macoutes (the huge presidential bodyguard), stands at the Health Minister's desk.

In the capital of Port-au-Prince, Ton Ton Macoutes – the word means bogeymen – swagger through the streets. They are above the law.

– are punishing him for failing in his religious duties.

If the man's tormentor is among the living he may be 'served with the left hand' – countered with black magic: but the dead and the *loa*, full of grandeur and power, can only 'be served with the right hand' and satisfied by a man's changed attitude to life. The Invisibles plague men because they also represent unused talents and energy locked up in the corpse of the past. Voodoo initiation – the subjection to a mock death and rebirth – transforms the Invisibles from persecutors into helpers. Again death figures as an illness. rebirth as a cure.

The novice's status depends on who. plagues him. If his ancestors are calling him to serve them, he must first serve the *loa*. So he must first find out which *loa* is 'in his head'. There are nations of *loa*, so called because they originated as gods of the various African tribes whose members came to Haiti. Slavery mixed them up so well that their descendants all came to be Haitian, but the gods retained their nationalities. These nations are called Rada, from the town of Arada in Dahomey; Wangol from Angola; Sinigia from Senegal; Congo, Ibo, Naga. Kaplaou and so on. There is also a truly Haitian nation, the revengeful Petro *loa*, born from the bitterness and misery of slavery. Families tend to serve the same nation 61

Ill-equipped laborers till Haiti's rich soil. Yet the island's wealth lies in the hands of a tiny elite: the people are desperately poor.

of *loa*. The novice may already know his *loa's* identity.

The *loa* affect both Man and Nature; for instance, Ogoun is the warlike blacksmith god, whose hammer is a thunderbolt; but he also controls the heads of the strong-minded. He may also patronize those who resent strong-mindedness in others, and is invoked to settle a disorder of the mind that makes a man get on badly with other people. And it opens the way for future *loa*. An initiate may become possessed by many *loa* during his lifetime.

Once accepted for initiation, the novice must buy the apparatus for the ceremony and acquire sacrificial animals. For one anxious week he rehearses, and on the sixth evening his head is washed to prepare him for his ordeal. On Saturday morning the initiation begins. The novice will be isolated in a room for the whole of the

Fighting cocks viciously attack each other. The sport attracts many spectators, many of them laying bets they can ill afford to lose.

Hats off for church! Sombreros perch in trees as a priest reads a prayer. Catholicism co-exists uneasily with voodooism.

A girl does the family laundry in the Rivière Froide. She washes her only shirt and puts it back on still wet.

next week. Before he enters the room where he is to be made ready for his *loa*, his companions chant songs, comparing him to a horse being saddled for its rider. Strips of shredded palm leaves are prepared for him to protect and to master him.

The atmosphere is full of tension and emotional excitement. Amid tears and a crescendo of chanting and wailing, the man is spun round and round, giving himself utterly into the hands of the people who surround him. He becomes giddier and giddier until he can no longer stand on his feet, and is suddenly and violently shoved into the chamber, to his ritual death.

The room is quiet and dimly lit. He lies on his left side, as he has been instructed, and takes some of the food that has been left for him – the white food that is always offered to the dead. During the week of his seclusion, the novice learns songs and prayers, secret passwords and gestures. He rigorously prepares himself for his possession by his *loa*, washing his head to calm his *gros bon ange*.

Outside, priests are preparing for his release. On the following Saturday they make a sacrifice of fowls, and fill a *govi* with parts of the birds, adding hair and nail clippings taken from the novice, symbols of the *gros bon ange*. They boil oil and flour together in a cauldron, and when the novice emerges from his room, swathed in a white sheet, a lump of this boiling mixture is pressed into his hand. Then he must pass through the flames himself, and return immediately to the darkened room.

Next day he is reborn and he comes out for good. It is a Sunday, the day of his baptism in magic. The drums strike up, the crowd begins to dance and the *loa* possesses its new servitor. But the man has been weakened by his ordeal; perhaps even injured. For 40 days he must convalesce, before he can be confirmed in his power.

He and the priest enter a dark room. The priest calls up the spirits of the ancestors which the novice wishes to serve. They are made to speak. Then they are put in a *govi* which, together with the one containing the novice's *gros bon ange*, is usually kept by the priest. The initiate is now a *hounsi canzo*, a spouse of the god.

Priests and priestesses are expert in many skills. They are gifted with 'la prise des yeux' – second sight – which allows them to remain conscious as they lull their followers into a coma by the rhythms of the *asson* – the gourd rattle. They have a detailed knowledge of rites, divination, exorcism and herbal medicine. They also know a great deal of the private lives of their parishioners, and can influence them – even for political ends. They are excellent managers, and combine the offices of priest, mayor, lawyer, doctor, counsellor and president of a self-help society. In Haiti there are no other institutions for social order, so the priests play an important role. Moreover, voodoo offers a fine opportunity for making money, and provides splendid and regular entertainment. It is all that Haitians have got.

Poor whites
Caribbean

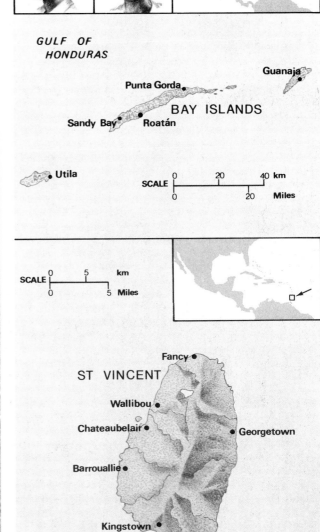

GULF OF
HONDURAS

Guanaja

Punta Gorda

BAY ISLANDS

Sandy Bay   Roatán

Utila

SCALE

| 0 | 20 | 40 km |
| 0 | 20 | Miles |

SCALE

| 0 | 5 | km |
| 0 | 5 | Miles |

Fancy

ST VINCENT

Wallibou

Chateaubelair

Georgetown

Barrouallie

Kingstown

Caribbean society still reflects the circumstances in which black and white immigrants first met there three centuries ago. White affluence and black poverty still dominate the lives of the descendants of planters and of slaves, but this is not the whole picture. Black poverty is now being alleviated; and while white affluence is still a source of social and political tension, it is rapidly changing emphasis as the old 'plantocracy' yields precedence and power to an increasing flood of easy-spending visitors, chiefly on vacation from the 65

The Bay Islands exemplify the
poor white communities of
the Caribbean, where the
planter and his slaves left
no room for a middle class.

United States or from Europe.

Then there are all the people in the Caribbean who cannot be classified as simply as 'black' or 'white' – the east Indians, the Chinese and Lebanese, and all the *gens de couleur* whose ancestry began with concubinage between masters and slaves, and who now occupy an ambiguous inter-racial position. And throughout the islands there are local communities, wholly European by origin, who have lived for a long time in poverty hardly distinguishable from that of their black neighbors. Only now are these 'poor whites' beginning to share in the improving prosperity of the West Indies.

Their story began when the early colonists of the islands found themselves confronted with a serious labor problem. The islands were potentially a source of immense wealth, but there was no manpower to develop the resources. The indigenous population – of Arawaks, Caribs, and Tanala Indians – had declined to a fraction of its former size under colonial pressures; and in any case, these Indians were never suitable as slaves. Before their problem was solved by large-scale development of the African slave-trade, the British and French had turned to Europe for white labor. In 17th century Europe this was easy: many migrants were considered undesirable in their own countries, while others – seeing few prospects at home – were eager to try their chances in a new country.

They came in quantity under three distinct arrangements, each of which marked them out for inferior status from the start. There was the system of indentured labor which, ideally, amounted to a kind of assisted immigration. Poor at home, a man or a woman would agree to be shipped out to some Caribbean island and to receive – eventually – a grant of land in that promising, prosperous New World. No payment would be asked for; but in return, to earn that new start, he or she would agree to labor or otherwise serve for a period that was usually three or four years.

In theory, this was not a bad method of colonization. In practice, there were many abuses. Indentured servants were often treated atrociously – sometimes worse than black slaves, since their masters had only a short-term interest in their well-being. They were often deceived about their prospects in the Caribbean and their recruitment was sometimes far from voluntary. Pressure was applied, and actual kidnapping for this purpose became a major problem in 17th century England. The system often broke down at the receiving end; disillusioned by what they found, perhaps reluctant to be there at all, many of these indentured servants took the first opportunity of escaping from the near-slavery into which they had fallen.

Despite these drawbacks, the system flourished: between 1654 and 1685, some ten thousand indentured servants sailed from Bristol alone to the British colonies on the mainland and in the West Indies. They were joined by people who came by the second system of importing labor, who were by no means the cream of England's population. One contemporary writer described Barbados as a dunghill onto which England cast forth its human garbage, its rogues and prostitutes. And this was the purpose of the transportation of convicts, which flourished alongside the system of indentured labor. The convicts were sent out in quantity, to the advantage (it was felt) of both sides. The home country was glad to be rid of people otherwise considered only fit for the gallows. The planters felt that convict labor was better than none, and might prove susceptible to moral reform and social rehabilitation. In this they were often disappointed: most of the convicts turned out to be reluctant workers and unreliable characters.

Finally, large numbers were deported to the West Indies during the political and religious upheavals of 17th century England – not because they were guilty of specific crimes, but because they were considered racially, socially or politically undesirable. Cromwell was chiefly responsible. He sent the few survivors of the massacre of Drogheda to Barbados. In 1651 he sold seven or eight thousand Scots, captured at the Battle of Worcester, to British plantations in the New World. In 1656 he imposed the same fate upon Irish girls and men, a thousand of each sex.

Some consciences were troubled by all this. It was widely felt that Christian people should not inflict slavery, or anything resembling it, upon one another – though it was different, of course, with pagan negroes. With more emphasis than plausibility, people found it necessary to say that these deportees and convicts were really very fortunate. Some were welcomed in the West Indies: Irish girls especially. 'It was a measure beneficial to Ireland,' wrote one English historian, 'which was thus relieved of a population that might trouble the planters (in Ireland); it was a benefit to the people removed, who might thus be made English and Christians; and a great benefit to the West India sugar planters, who desired

(Opposite) Impossible to marry into the 'plantocracy', unthinkable to marry negroes, whites of forced labor stock have kept aloof – but poor.

It is every boy's ambition to have a boat of his own. Fish is a vital source of food. Bar chicken, there is no meat, though coconuts abound.

The ancestors of this man climbing to cut a coconut might have been among the 8,000 Scots Cromwell deported after the Battle of Worcester.

the men and boys for their bondmen, and the women and Irish girls in a country where they had only maroon women and full negresses to solace them.'

The long-term prospects were, unfortunately, limited for most of these people. The indentured laborers had commonly been induced to come by the promise of land when their time was served. But most West Indian islands are small and the land was simply not available. As the sugar-economy developed, it polarized the society of the islands, leaving little room for laborers and small farmers of white origin.

Indentured laborers, convicts and deportees found it increasingly hard to establish a footing in the society and economy of the Caribbean, and employment was hard to find. They could not work on the sugar plantations for there African slaves were cheaper and worked harder. They could not promote themselves, except in rare instances, into the closed circles of the plantocracy or the professions. There was no room for a white middle class.

As the 18th century proceeded, the people descended from the previous century's intake of indentured laborers, convicts and deportees found themselves elbowed aside by the incoming flood of Africans, and driven into

Many St Vincent whites came from England as indentured workers in the 17th century. Others were sentenced to transportation.

the position of incurable poverty, passed on to their children and descendants, which remains today.

In England and in the Caribbean, the authorities were aware of this situation, and were worried by the growing numbers of Africans. They made attempts to keep up the flow of indentured servants by law, but economic reality was too strong and well before the 18th century was over the system ended completely. At

Socially some poor whites have compromised with their isolation. The Davis children, for example, show traces of a negro forbear.

various times, they also made attempts to do something for this new class of poor whites. When the French part of St Kitts was ceded to Britain in 1712, it was proposed that some part of these 20,000 acres of land – the worst part – should be handed over in ten-acre plots to the poor whites. Unfortunately, the power of money overruled this limited but excellent plan: the land was sold to the highest bidders, and the poor whites remained landless. Later, in 1781, a rather desperate plan was established on Barbados to give the poor whites an occupation by teaching them to spin and weave: very little came of it.

The outcome was inevitable. All over the Caribbean, on this island and that, small groups of Europeans – chiefly English and French – found themselves coerced into the status and the economic position of negro freedmen; with a sense of grievance against both races, they withdrew into themselves and into an inward-looking existence. Marriage with the wealthy plantocracy was impossible; with the negroes it was unthinkable. And the same went for all social relationships. The poor whites kept to themselves, proud and dignified in their poverty, marrying their own sort within limited areas, suffering therefore the slow penalties of physical and psychological isolation and in-breeding.

Groups of them still exist today in many parts of the Caribbean, stranded here and there by the tide of history, like fish stranded in a rock-pool when the tide goes out; wearing similar rags and living in similar shacks to poor black West Indians, they are distinguishable from them only by their color. But they preserve a proud, fierce independence and sense of identity, although officially their existence is hardly recognized. From time to time, the traveler to Barbados – its very name a word of terror in 17th century England – will see blue-eyed and fair-haired white men, working in the fields or resting in the doorways of wretched shacks. These are the Redlegs, alternatively known as 'the Mean Whites.' Some are descended from convicts, but most of them are descended from the followers of the Duke of Monmouth, deported by order of the notorious Judge Jeffreys after the Battle of Sedgemoor in 1685. Some, too, are descendants of Cromwell's Scottish and (especially) Irish victims. The distinctive Barbadian speech has a definitely Irish ring to it, while some students also detect in it the tones of Somerset and Devon and Dorset, the home-counties of so many who followed Monmouth.

These Redlegs, so mixed in their origins, have, until recently, led a pitiable existence. Their poverty was unrelieved and hopeless. Unlike the black peoples of the island, they have taken little part in public affairs. Many of them – especially some of Scottish origin – have moved to nearby Grenada and St Vincent where they have considerably improved their condition, although they are still identified as 'poor whites.'

A happier destiny, perhaps, is that of the 'Bretons' who may have come originally from Brittany – who live on the Iles des Saints, six small islands to the south of Guadeloupe. They now speak neither French nor Breton, but creole, the Afro-Gaulish *patois* of the black population. Here and there due to recent intermarriage, negro features are visible among them, but most are of pure European stock, fair-complexioned, brown-haired or blond, their eyes blue or grey, their features fine and aquiline. Many of them are good-looking, tall, and healthy; but centuries of in-breeding have resulted in a distressingly heavy incidence of disease, notably elephantiasis, leprosy and insanity.

But they are not an unhappy people. They are fishermen and skilled boat-builders: every morning, the channel between Guadeloupe and the islands is full of their distinctively-rigged sailing craft. Life is easy for them: fishing is over by the early afternoon, and the rest of their day tends to be dominated by rum and argument. Their conversational manner is violent, and quarrels are frequent: isolation has conferred a chronic immaturity upon these people. But they are generous, charitable and honest; as brave as open-boat fishermen usually need to be; and they have an enviable gift for enjoying life. On the other side of the Caribbean is Utila – one of the Bay Islands ceded in 1859 by Great Britain to Honduras. Already it had an English population: the first English family settled there in 1836, and now there are about one thousand Utilans, all English-speaking, all – by temperament as well as origin – Englishmen living under a foreign flag, and all poor. Their island's precarious economy depends upon fish and coconuts: there is little livestock, and fresh meat is a rare luxury.

Towards this proud remnant, intolerant of strangers and resentful of negroes, the government of Honduras implements a policy based chiefly upon indifference, coupled with a faint desire that they should be assimilated: all education, for example, has to be in Spanish. But the stubborn Utilans fight to the last ditch, speaking their own language in their homes and teaching it to their children, while clinging to ideas and attitudes that are English by origin, though long ago discarded in England. Theirs is a healthy life: heart disease and cancer are rare among them, and most live to a ripe old age. But their existence is in jeopardy for they show greater signs of in-breeding than other groups; and most able young people tend to emigrate to seek better prospects elsewhere.

In the Caribbean, life is changing rapidly, and rising prosperity and better communications may finally end the isolation of 'poor white' groups. They will, possibly, be assimilated and lose their passionate sense of being different; perhaps they will lose their poverty too. But in the meantime, one can feel certain sympathy for people so unexpectedly stranded and isolated by the unpredictable tides of history, so blindly but bravely determined to retain their various identities, and their beloved inheritances.

69

People of Martinique and Guadeloupe

The first thing which a visitor to the French Antilles will notice is the immense and immediate difference in feel between Martinique and Guadeloupe on the one hand and the English-speaking parts of the Caribbean on the other. Everywhere on these islands French is spoken, with a curious intonation that stems from the habit of changing all the 'r' sounds to 'w'. A Creole of Martinique or Guadeloupe will, for example, describe the traditional gaily colored silk overskirt or 'grande robe' as a 'gwan wobe.' The local patois derived from French can be quite unintelligible to the stranger.

And yet, the Lesser Antilles were first found and occupied by the Spanish: they were discovered by Christopher Columbus on his second voyage in 1493. He gave them names derived from the circumstances of the moment: Guadeloupe because he had worshipped at the shrine of Mary of Guadeloupe before he set out; the Isles of the Saints because All Saints' Day had just passed; Marie Galante after his flagship; Dominica because the first time he set eyes on it was on a Sunday.

It was probably at about this time, or just before, that the original Indian inhabitants – the Arawak – were driven from the Lesser Antilles by Carib Indians who invaded the islands from the Amazon basin. Most of the survivors left the Lesser Antilles, and settled in the Greater Antilles. In Martinique and Guadeloupe the Arawak are known only through archaeology.

The aristocrats of Arawak society were permitted special houses, food, titles and signs of their rank, while most of the work was done by a peasant class of commoners and captive slaves. Poor soldiers, they were easily defeated by the fierce, more egalitarian Caribs, who chased them as far as Jamaica and Hispaniola.

Carib expansion was halted by the coming of the Spaniards who largely controlled the Caribbean for most of the 16th century. But the Spanish were increasingly challenged by the British and the Dutch, and, by the end of the century, by the French as well. The French decided to settle in Martinique at the beginning of the 17th century as part of a general policy to reduce Spanish influence. For the first few years of the century, relations between the French and the Caribs were fairly peaceful, but after the expedition of d'Enambuc in 1625 the Caribs became convinced that the French intended to destroy them. They were about to attack the settlers but were forestalled, and themselves beaten. Peaceful co-existence or at least 'armed truce' lasted until the middle of the century when relations sharply deteriorated and in 1660 a treaty between the French, the English and the Indians, gave St Vincent and Dominica to the Indians and left the newcomers in possession of Guadeloupe and Martinique.

There was constant rivalry between French and English from the end of the 17th and throughout the 18th century. After the Napoleonic War, Guadeloupe was ceded to the French in 1814, and Martinique in 1815,

(Top) Shaded by umbrellas, smallholders sell fruit and tomatoes in Point à Pitre, Guadeloupe, during the sugar-cane slack season.

(Center) Prosperous St Pierre, Martinique, with its fine French-style residences was rebuilt after the disastrous eruption of Mt Pelée in 1902.

(Bottom) The islands are officially not colonies but departments of France. Many islanders feel French, think French – and dress French.

and they have remained French ever since. They became *départements* of France after World War II and continue to send their Deputies to the National Assembly in Paris. The Deputy for Martinique is the famous poet Aimé Césaire, whose incisive and impassioned work has influenced the evolution of the idea of *négritude*.

To most, the French Antilles have always been – and still are – France. The Martiniquais think of themselves as Frenchmen. When some Martiniquais asked the Trinidad writer V S Naipaul if he was English and he replied that he came from Trinidad, he was gently accused of splitting hairs.

Tourists from the US and Europe like the 'French' shops with their Dior ties, Hermès scarves, Chanel perfumes and gourmet foods flown in from France. The newspapers are almost exclusively French and come by air and the Martiniquais poet, Aimé Césaire, is rightly considered a major figure of French literature. But if much of this is advantageous or at worst harmless, there is a reverse to the coin which is less clearly beneficial. Prejudices which in France itself are social but surmountable have, in this tropical world where so much tends to be exaggerated, become harder, more inflexible, more racial. The metropolitan bourgeois lives in a hierarchical world with a definite view of class distinction and rigid rules of behavior. In a large society he will find room for movement and change; there will be enough elasticity in the system to prevent it becoming too oppressive, hidebound or rigid. In a small society this flexibility is even more necessary, but in Martinique and Guadeloupe it is lacking. In the early work of Césaire, published from the late 1930s onwards, it is possible to see described – indeed decried – the basic problems of social structure which continue to bedevil Guadeloupe as well as Martinique. Césaire's two worlds of 'black' and 'white' – white representing capital, dominance and privilege, black representing labor, subordination and disadvantage – are still the basis of the islands' society, although color is no longer the only criterion of class. Aimé Césaire himself, apostle of the concept of *négritude*, black culture, casts himself firmly among the 'black' world.

As the economic system suffers from inertia, people easily feel frustrated or oppressed. The feeling might be dismissed as inevitable in the purely colonial situation where white Frenchmen effectively ruled black 'subjects', but people's lives have changed little in the 25 years since Martinique became a full *département,* and the feelings which Césaire expressed in 1938 are still felt by many of the poorer people on the islands: there were race riots in the late 1950s and early 1960s and there is still tension.

Beneath the French urban style of life there is a much lower standard of living with far fewer opportunities for the majority of the population. But serious suffering is not common. When the islands became French *départements* France also extended to the islands her system of social security; nearly everyone has access to free medical and pharmaceutical care. Supplements are paid to both salaried and lower-paid workers to help them support their families. But the life of the peasant remains conspicuously different and harder compared with the life of the townspeople.

The economy of the islands is based on the great staples of Caribbean agricultural production: sugar and rum, bananas and pineapples. The factories which process the sugar cane are few and almost entirely white-owned. The estates which produce cane, bananas and pineapples are predominantly owned by whites, who also have a large share in the import–export businesses and in retail shops. So, as elsewhere in the Caribbean, whites are still firmly at the top of the social tree. Mulattos command a large section of the professional occupations and also predominate in government posts and other white-collar occupations in the towns.

But the majority of the population is black. And while there are certainly blacks in all sections of the society, nearly all of them live in the country. During the six months of the cane harvest they work in fields or in factories which process the cane. For the other six months they are at best underemployed, looking after their smallholdings in the country where they raise fruit and vegetables for household consumption or for sale in the local markets, or unemployed.

In these circumstances the towns are inevitably attractive. In town there is a possibility of work as a docker – mainly loading sacks of sugar or sticks of bananas. Some of the poor rural black people manage to find jobs in factories, some in shops and there are always opportunities as drivers or in tourism. Unfortunately there are less job opportunities in the towns than there are people who come specially to fill them. Many hopeful employees end up joining that disappointed crowd of workless which is to be found in almost any Caribbean town. The Communist vote is often high in the French Antilles. However much the strong Communist sympathies reflect the general political situation in metropolitan France, in the islands they are stimulated by their own fundamental pressures and conflicts. The people of Guadeloupe and Martinique are convinced of the need for change.

Both islands have suffered volcanic eruption; Guadeloupe, last in 1843 when several towns were destroyed, and Martinique in 1902 when St Pierre, the capital at that time, was destroyed with its population of over 30,000 except for one criminal who survived in a thick-walled cell. Hurricanes also have taken their toll. Economic development or at least social improvement may come in time to prevent a future political disaster. It should not be forgotten that during the French Revolution Guadeloupe had its own terror (on a small scale) and executed 1,200 royalists on its own little guillotine.

People of Newfoundland St Pierre and Miquelon

From the ice-free harbors on
the south-west coast,
Newfoundlanders fish from
dories all the year and
in all weather conditions.

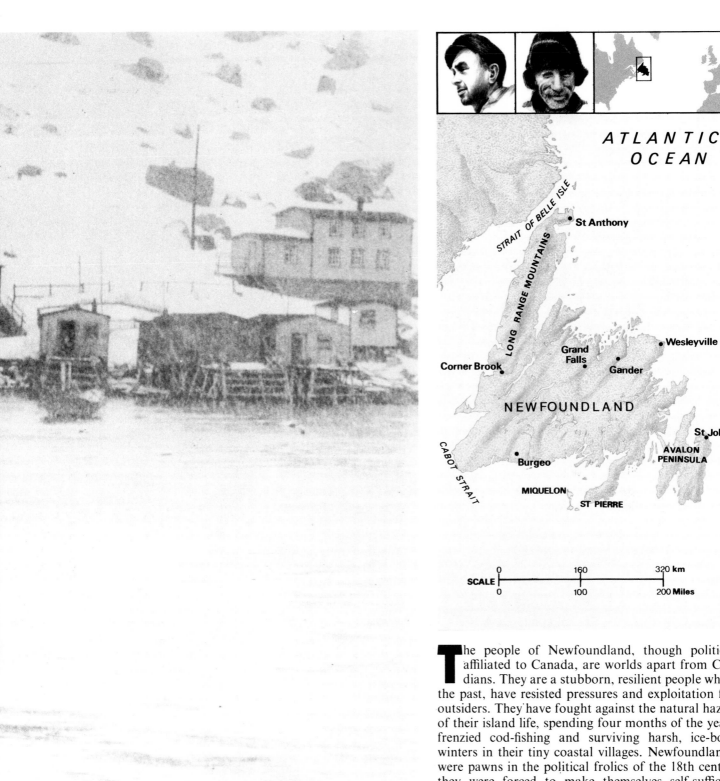

The map shows:

ATLANTIC
OCEAN

STRAIT OF BELLE ISLE

St Anthony

LONG RANGE MOUNTAINS

Wesleyville

Grand
Falls

Corner Brook

Gander

NEWFOUNDLAND

CABOT STRAIT

St Johns

AVALON
PENINSULA

Burgeo

MIQUELON

ST PIERRE

SCALE
0 — 160 — 320 km
0 — 100 — 200 Miles

The people of Newfoundland, though politically affiliated to Canada, are worlds apart from Canadians. They are a stubborn, resilient people who, in the past, have resisted pressures and exploitation from outsiders. They have fought against the natural hazards of their island life, spending four months of the year in frenzied cod-fishing and surviving harsh, ice-bound winters in their tiny coastal villages. Newfoundlanders were pawns in the political frolics of the 18th century; they were forced to make themselves self-sufficient. There was little help for them from the English government who, at one time, instructed their Navy to destroy settlements which sprang up on the island. Families in the villages along 6,000 miles of coastline grew up hardy 73

A man slithers forward over the dangerous melting ice. He has a gun. His victims are seals and their young . . . hunted for their pelts.

and independent. To this day, since the 20th century has swept away so many of their traditional ways, these characteristics distinguish Newfoundlanders.

The vast island of Newfoundland is rocky and barren on its coast. Inland, the bogs and forests do not make it either an inviting land, or a land to cultivate. The weather is harsh: great winds, rain and heavy seas constantly batter the rugged coastline. But these same seas are the source of the island's wealth. For centuries the island has been irresistible to fishermen; the shallow coastal waters are full of fish. The story of the people of this island is really the story of her fishermen; her history is closely interwoven with the history of her fisheries. In the 15th century John Cabot made his celebrated voyage across the Atlantic and with this, and his discovery of the island of Newfoundland, the huge fishing potential of the Labrador coast and the shallow continental shelf was first recognized. And within a few years its exploitation had begun. Soon there were fortunes to be made, and settlements on the island to be won and lost.

The fishermen who followed John Cabot were not the first to exploit the island's resources. As long ago as 4,000 BC, Eskimos had crossed the narrow straits of Belle Isle from the Labrador mainland and settled in the northern peninsula. Woodland Beothuck Indians, related to mainland Indians, also crossed to the islands and lived in the forests and around the lakes. Nor were the 15th century fishermen the first Europeans on the island. Around 1,000 AD there were Norsemen who by design or by accident crossed the Atlantic to Newfoundland's shores. Perhaps because of hostility from the Indians, but probably because of the harshness of the island's environment the Norsemen's settlements did not survive. For the new settlers 600 years later, the weather was as fierce, the coast as unfriendly and the land as unyielding; little had changed over the years.

This time it was planters, and deserters from English fishing fleets sent to catch the great cod shoals, who settled on the island. Their main problem was not the weather which they could cope with, but their rivalry with the fishermen who came seasonally from England. The merchant fishermen of western England disliked colonization because they resented the settlers' advantage in sites for curing the catch. And they had the support of the British government. Fishing was a large commercial interest which brought much wealth to the country, and

Grandfather was a fisherman. But father is a logger — working in a shanty camp in the forest for Newfoundland's big paper making industry.

75

An islander triumphantly holds up a shearwater he has shot. These birds, if caught when young, are fat and thought very good to eat.

An old-style Newfoundland
party — 'a time' — gets
under way as the men let
themselves go in a jig,
admired by the women.

Newfoundland joined Canada
only in 1949. Traditions are
fiercely their own, and many
of the people remain
hardy fishermen.

An abandoned cemetery stands
on Hunt's isle. Lack of soil
made it impossible to dig
deep, so the coffins were
placed on the surface.

fishermen were even awarded temporary authority over Newfoundlanders. The earliest rule that Newfoundland knew was by the 'Fishing Admirals', who were the captains of the first fishing vessel to reach port in the spring. They became the official dispensers of justice and the system was not replaced until the 18th century.

The fishing charter of 1634 directed that all fishing ships should carry one apprentice for every four trained sailors – and so assured, while encouraging the development of the fishing industry in Newfoundland, a steady stream of new naval recruits as a foundation of naval strength. The British government actively discouraged colonization. They forbade settlement within six miles of the Newfoundland coast – except in parts of the eastern Avalon peninsula – and directed that the fishing ships carry no passengers or potential settlers. This policy was enforced by the navy which patrolled the coast with orders to destroy all illegal settlements. Masters of all ships were placed under heavy bond to return to England in the fall with every man who had shipped with them in the spring.

But it was impossible to enforce a strict six-mile rule or to prevent colonization. The permanent colony grew. In 1728 the captain of the naval convoy that accompanied the fishing fleet as a protection against pirates and enemy ships was appointed to administer the law. But in the absence of the fleet in the winter months, resident justices were invested with this authority. The result was periods of alternating disorder and stern repression. By 1774 there were 15,000 settlers on the island and only 9,000 seasonal fishermen. For the settlers these early years were a time of great hardship. Most islanders were extremely poor. The great profits of the fishing industry – which in 1804 brought in 600,000 hundred-weight of fish and 100,000 seals – went to the merchants of Europe. To add to the troubles of the Newfoundland people, French and American privateers made raids on their settlements. And by the 18th century, these and Spanish and Portuguese vessels were intruding on Newfoundland fishing grounds.

In 1763, in exchange for two settlements in Canada, the British handed over sovereignty to the French of two of Newfoundland's islands – St Pierre and Miquelon. These two islands, off the south coast of Newfoundland, gave the French fishing fleets depots where their catch could be salted before shipping back to France. In 1793 the French settlements were destroyed by a British fleet, and the settlers were returned to France. But 20 years later the islands were handed back to the French, and French and Breton settlers returned. St Pierre, the only town on the two islands, was crowded again during spring and fall when the Breton fishermen from the fleets would land and enjoy the hospitality and smuggled brandy of the islanders who today, in their speech, preserve many 18th century French idioms.

In Newfoundland, the illicit settlement continued.

The island has 6,000 miles of coastline littered with small hidden coves, inlets and isolated headlands. The settlers made their homes in these places, protected by rough but shallow coastal waters – which were inaccessible to the English, French and American ships and almost impossible to reach from inland. Only here could the settlers, often fugitives and always in breach of the law, avoid arrest.

All around the island hundreds of these small settlements sprang up. The settlers had to live through long, cold winters with heavy snow and arctic ice. From their rocky, shallow coast they had to fish in wild, angry seas with their own boats. There were few compensations. The enforced isolation denied the people access to the clergy, medical care, schools, markets and any communication with their former homes in the outside world. They were, in every sense, cut off. Catholic and Protestant sectarianism tore the smallest communities apart.

Without priest or clergy, religious worship in the outport fishing villages was largely conducted by lay preachers. Folk-lore and traditions sustained beliefs – but the isolated people were subject also to flagrant abuses by outsiders. Promises made to them were ignored. Economic and political liberation was not forthcoming. So strangers were regarded with suspicion; outsiders were synonymous with malevolence. All this had wide ramifications in the superstitions of the islanders. Many of their traditions had come from Ireland and England, and were preserved as the islanders clung to their old ways and resisted the changes brought by outsiders. Newfoundlanders, for example, continue the Mummers' plays of Christmastide which, in the old world, have long since died out.

The settlers in these outports and coastal villages were effectively outside the law. But eventually schooners from St Johns, the capital of Newfoundland, visited them to trade salt, canvas, twine, rope, molasses, tea and flour with the villagers' fish. The trade was not however on the villagers' terms. They had to sell their fish for what the schooners' merchants would give them and buy at the merchants' prices. For just one annual visit the outport people labored the year round. It was their only means of trade as well as their sole link with the outside world. The trade gave fat profits to the merchants from St Johns, and others from England, but the Newfoundland villagers made barely enough to live on. The system was a yoke about their necks.

The island did not establish trading posts of its own until the 19th century. The trading posts which were set up in the outport villages sold a limited range of goods, but they were accessible, always there, and their prices were fair. Now the outport settlements were no longer illegal, they had nothing to fear from the authorities, and they began to expand. But until villages and towns were connected by roads the outports remained dependent on the schooners' visits to sell fish. Still prices were fixed. 77

The provincial parliament
building dominates St Johns.
Though the settlers came in
the 1600s, they had no
civil governor until 1825.

Bargaining was useless: the villager who tried to resist the merchants' monopoly seldom did so for long.

It was under these extreme circumstances that Newfoundland outport society evolved. Well into the 20th century all of Newfoundland's 1,200 settlements were on the coast; there were none in the island's interior. Each of them developed separately, adapting in its own way to its own conditions. Each depended entirely on fishing to keep it alive. Fishing, and preparing for fishing, was the overwhelming activity, and chief interest of village life.

Arctic ice and the heavy seas along much of Newfoundland's coast mean the fishermen are unable to fish for more than four months of the year. The fishing season in Newfoundland is like a farmer's short harvest: the catch comes all at once. The cod traps must be set, hauled, and emptied quickly. The fish must be headed, gutted, split and salted quickly. And all must be ready for the schooner's visit in the fall. Preparing the catch would keep the entire community in a constant state of activity during those four months.

Talking of fish among villagers meant talking of cod. Those who fished for salmon or lobster were not referred to as fishermen. Close to the shore, the cod were trapped, but further out – as far as six miles – they were netted or hooked. Inshore trap fishing involved a crew of three or five men in a 32-foot boat. These crews were made up of fathers and sons and sometimes male cousins. Wives, sisters and unmarried daughters made up what was called the 'shore crowd' – who processed the fish after it was landed. Women never went out in the boats, but their job was so important and held in such esteem that a man

The only road which spans the rugged, harsh and barren landscape of the island is the Trans-Canada Highway finished in 1968.

(Center) A fine catch of caplin is laid out to dry. It is caught in great quantities and eaten either fresh or dried.

Since the 1920s, manufacture of paper has been a major industry. Timber is floated down the rivers to be pulped in gigantic mills.

In 1813 the isle of St Pierre
was returned to France as a
port for their fishing fleet.
Today their speech has many
18th century French idioms.

The islanders of St Pierre
are stubbornly Gallic. Here
a group of men enjoy
playing the traditional
French game of boules.

without a wife helping in the 'shore crowd' was given a lesser share of the catch. In the short time that the fish were plentiful, a crew hauled traps three or four times a day – an 18 hour shift was common for both fishermen and their women-folk.

A great deal of gear was necessary to equip a boat and crew. The cod traps – huge nets, long ropes and moorings – weighed many hundreds of pounds. As a boat, with all its fittings and maintenance, was too much for one man to afford, it was a family investment – and this reinforced the need for family involvement in the fishing. Kinsmen were bound together by bonds more elemental than blood – for families could only survive by sharing the labors of fishing. They lived and worked together; fathers, sons and brothers stayed in the same village, but sisters and daughters might marry out of it.

For generations the cycle of fishing families remained the same. When a son had saved enough to buy his own boat, and his own sons were old enough to help with the fishing, he would break away and establish new fishing territories, with separate wharfs and buildings. The cycle began again. Over the years the waterfronts of most villages became crowded. In some places overgrown communities were forced to split up and groups resettled further along the coast. Where there were deep water harbors, schooners were built which then spent the summer fishing off the Labrador coast, bringing home their salted catch each fall.

Soon the months of the fishing season were over. The gear was taken off the boats and dried. The boats were pulled up and the fishing stages and bridges (tiny shacks built out over the water where the processing was done) all taken down to avoid the crushing seas of the fall and the ice of winter and spring. Every new season the stages and bridges had to be re-erected – it was a lot of work. In the fall the men turned to repairs and agriculture. Grass was cut and stored to feed the few cattle and horses throughout the winter; then the men spent several weeks in the forests cutting timber for fuel, enough to last them through the coming year. The wood was necessary also for repairing or building a new house, boat and furniture. The women spent the winter knitting new pieces for the cod traps and nets. By the time the winter was full upon Newfoundland, trees had to be pulled out by horse or dog sled, then dragged over the frozen ground. It was a time for trapping the foxes, ermines, beavers and rabbits; and hunting animals like caribou and moose.

In the early spring, when the break-up of the arctic ice packs began, North Atlantic seals bore their young on the floes. Newfoundland men took to hunting the seals. It was called the 'seal fishery' and was a potentially lucrative season. But it was also fraught with the danger of moving about in the ice floes and most communities had their tragedies when a hunter lost his life in the freezing water. The thaw meant the villagers could again dig their gardens in which potatoes, turnips, cabbages and other root vegetables were grown. With dried fish, moose, rabbit and wild berries, these vegetables formed the bulk of the islanders' diet. Through the winter they needed a great store of food; and even in the summer, when fishing took up most of the day, they would eat food that had been stored since the winter. In Newfoundland, the people lived in harmony with the season. What their island provided they took and made use of: they had little else besides.

In the early 20th century Newfoundland first attracted the eyes of industrialists. After World War I the island became strategically important. Now another change, another adversity, was forced upon the islanders. They found themselves in a new environment that demanded further adaptation on their part. The advent of industry brought new, and sometimes hostile, forces to bear on the island's society.

In the 1920s the first pulp and paper mills were established on the island. The stunted firs and spruce trees were ideal for the manufacture of paper. Great tracts of land were leased to the paper companies and because of the low prices fish were fetching, many of the islanders were absorbed into new occupations as full-time loggers. They left their families in the coastal villages and moved to shanty camps in the forest. For much of the year they were away, cutting timber and hauling it to the lakes and rivers from where it could be floated down to the gigantic pulp mills.

Other industries were also developed: the mining of iron ore, copper, lead and zinc. On the outbreak of World War II America built military bases on the island – and more of the islanders became wage-laborers. In 1949 Newfoundland was led into confederation with Canada with the call to 'burn your boats – there will be three jobs for every man', and with this Newfoundlanders entered another era. Industrial capitalism has today come almost completely to supplant the simple fishing economy of the island. Fresh fish plants have been built and fishermen are encouraged to shift from inshore trap fishing to factory-dragger operations up to 200 miles offshore. Other nations, including Russia and Japan, send fleets of trawlers to exploit the offshore grounds. By the early 1970s the cod stocks had been drastically reduced. Inshore fishing has become progressively less rewarding; and it is more and more difficult to make a living. Islanders now fish for lobster and salmon as well – 'fish' soon meant more than just cod.

The people of Newfoundland are moving away from the coastal villages. Small fishing ventures are declining; traditional family groupings are no longer essential to survival. Rather the people are forced to move to lumber camps, or to St Johns. Hundreds of small communities become a few large towns. Newfoundlanders, whose history is bound up with the sea, no longer wrestle with its capricious nature. Now their battle is with the turbulence of industry.

Faroe Islanders
North-east Atlantic

FAROE ISLANDS

Eide•
Kvannesund •
Arnefjord •
BORDOY
EYSTUROY
Kvalvig•
Skalebotn
Vestmanhavn •
STREYMOY
VAGAR
Sorvags
Thorshavn •

ATLANTIC

OCEAN

SANDOY

Trangisvag
SUDUROY

SCALE 0   10   20   30 km
       0   10   Miles

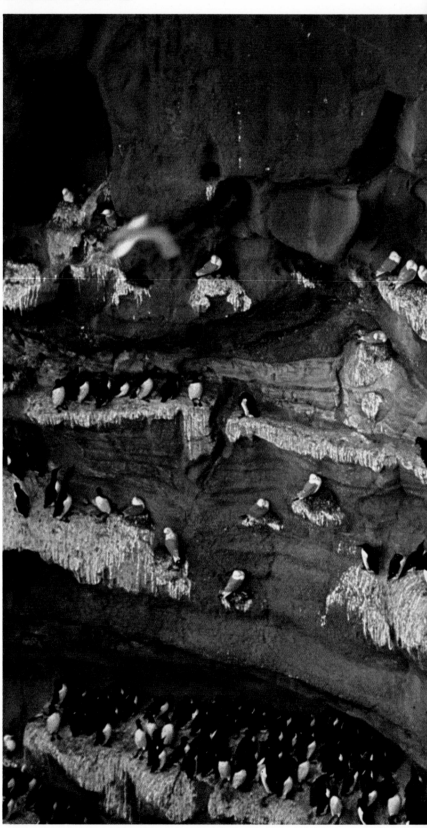

Outside the fjords, in the rolling waters of the north Atlantic, a few fishing-boats are at work together. Skilfully, by efficient traditional methods the men deploy their lines and nets. Already the fish are piling up in the bottom of the boats – cod, saithe, halibut, herrings, as the place and season may provide.

One man suddenly tenses, shades his eyes, and then wildly shouts the word of glory, excitement and sudden wealth: 'Grindaboth!' The other men look up in disbelief and then in delight; at once a flag is hoisted and the other boats close in.

On shore, on these craggy and remote Faroe Islands, people see the flag and the purposeful gathering of the boats, and at once the message flies around – 'Grinda-

A Faroese man is lowered to
gather guillemot eggs — 500
feet down the cliff side —
which will provide the
islander with much food.

both!' Today the message is flashed by priority telephone-call but in the old days it was by the lighting of beacons. People stop work at once: the children are let out of school, and even the Løgting – the Council or Parliament of the Faroes – suspends its sitting if the cry has gone up on that side of the islands. Everybody within reasonable distance wants to have his share of the excitement and the wealth, and the crowds gather by the shore or along the harborside to watch.

The word which generates such high excitement comes from *grind*, the name of the pilot or caaing whale – a creature once of enormous importance, and important still, to the economy of these islands where meat is scarce. That fisherman had spotted a school of these whales. By now the hunt is on.

The whales must be driven towards some gently-shelving bay, or into the harbor at Torshávn, the capital, so that they can be stranded and slaughtered there. The boats which first spotted the school are joined by others, and soon a captain of the *grindadráp*, the whale-hunt, is appointed. His commands have the force of law: but long custom with the desire to perform well is what governs men's conduct at this strenuous moment.

So now, under the command of the *grindaformathur*, the captain, the boats form a crescent behind the whales and very gently drive them forward. It is a delicate task, and the wind and the tide and the time of day create complex tactical problems. Sometimes the whales escape, and are not always rounded up again. But more usually the *grindadráp* proceeds according to plan. While the people throng the shore in mounting excitement, the whales come nearer, with the boats behind them: then, at a carefully chosen moment, one leading whale is speared in his hinder parts and sharply bounds forward. The rest of the school follow, and are at once floundering in shallow water, blinded by churned-up sand and mud and very soon by blood as well; an army of men descend upon them with sharp and terrible weapons, and the butchery begins. Few of the whales escape.

It is a scene of carnage, quite unlike anything that could be called sport. But whaling is in the blood of the Faroese, and a successful *grindadráp* is not only wildly exciting and often dangerous for the men who take part, but also a spectacle and a delight and blessing for all the people. Even the women and children throw themselves into it unreservedly, despite the blood and the smell.

When it is over, and the people give themselves up to a night-long dance and festivity to celebrate their good fortune, there may be sixty or a hundred dead whales to be divided and shared out according to an ancient and complicated system of rules and priorities only paralleled by the equally complex Faroese system of land tenure. The Faroese are a tough people, descended from the Vikings who occupied the islands in the 10th century. Over the centuries they have learnt that in such condi-

tions rugged individualism needs to be tempered with give-and-take, with careful attention to fair shares and to rule and precedent. Whale-meat and land are both precious, and every man's rights must be respected.

The Faroes are a close group of more than twenty islands, seventeen of which are inhabited: the total area is about 540 square miles. For many years they had close links with Norway. After that the country was united to Denmark in 1380 and came increasingly under Danish influence. From 1816 onwards, they had the status of a Danish province: during World War II they were occupied by the British, and in the course of their efforts to keep the British Isles supplied with fish, they lost a higher proportion of their manhood than any of the combatant powers lost in that war. Since 1948 they have been a self-governing community of about 40,000 people within the kingdom of Denmark.

These islands are bleak and forbidding; their gaunt beauty does not appeal to all. Most of their area is mountainous and desolate, often rising abruptly from the sea with terrifying cliffs and crags. But at some places along the shore, there are patches of low-lying land, less than 4 per cent of the whole land area, which can be cultivated. Here human settlement is possible, though always arduous. Historically, it has always depended upon three factors: the possibility of landing a boat, the possibility of building, and the presence of arable land. Developed land is known as the *bøur* or cultivated in-field of the village. Sheep and cattle are pastured here; hay is gathered and dried and stored in the short, cool Faroes summer; potatoes and other roots are grown; crops are rotated carefully.

The traditional farms and houses of the Faroe Islands were built to suit local conditions and from locally-available materials; stone, turf, and driftwood. Structures were always low because of the high winds, and the various buildings of a farm were separated from each other. One central room was called the *rögstue*, 'the room with a fire' – its smoke escaping through a hole in the roof – and this was the communal room, where the family lived together and where on the open fire beneath the smoke-hole the cooking was done. There were benches on which people could sit in the daytime, and alcoves along the wall in which they could sleep at night. There was usually a somewhat grander room as well, only used on special occasions: this was comfortably furnished and had no hole in the roof, and was named from the fact that it actually had glass in the windows – until recently a rare luxury on the islands.

Agricultural land is so scarce and conditions are generally so arduous that there has to be mutual help and a careful adjustment of interests. And so, over the centuries, the Faroese have developed a system of land tenure which rivals in complexity the system governing the distribution of whale-meat after a *grindadráp*. In Catholic days some of the land was Church land and is

The Faroes, once the home of
Irish monks, were overrun by
Vikings in the 8th century.
Their Lutheran descendants
now speak an Old Norse tongue.

A bride and bridegroom wear
traditional clothes – the man,
a coat with silver buttons
and waistcoat, the girl, a
gown with brooch and belt.

85

The real wedding festivities
begin the day after at noon.
A long and lavish feast,
lasting seven hours, is then
followed by a crowded dance.

Drinking is restricted: wines and spirits come from Denmark and you can get a liquor permit only by showing you have paid your taxes.

Grindaboth! A whale hunt nears its climax as a school of pilot whales is driven to shallow water where they will be stranded and slaughtered.

One of the few Faroese occupations that does not involve the sea is spinning wool which will be knitted into thick, oiled sweaters.

Whaling is an important industry for the Faroese, but the larger whales, like this 72 foot fin whale, are in danger of extinction.

(Bottom) Less than an hour after the *grindadrap* the celebrations begin. There will be night-long dancing, drinking and singing.

(Left) Stranded and blinded by sand and blood, few whales escape slaughter at this stage of the *grindadrap*. In 15 minutes the carnage is over.

now held directly from the Danish Crown, and some is held from the village communities. Farms that are worked on this basis can be maintained as fairly large units. Privately-owned land, however, falls under the provisions of a law which decrees that after the owner's death, it must be divided equally among all his children. This leads to a progressive fragmentation of the holding, as under the *Code Napoléon*, so that an individual's land may today consist of many widely-scattered patches in different places, commonly long and narrow in shape, like the strip-holdings in medieval England.

By some standards, the Faroese are a crude, primitive people. They certainly have a hard life, even though a degree of modernity has come upon them, bringing its questionable benefits. But they are great masters of the arts of living and of courtesy. Their homes are lively and clean and gay; they enjoy bright colors and the pleasures of dancing; and towards the guest they are generous to a fault. The visitor to these islands may be disconcerted by all the food offered to him: a couple or more roast puffins, still complete in their skins, may repel him initially, though he will find their meat delicious when he takes the plunge. But he may still find *skerpikjøt* too leathery for his tastes: most of us would prefer our mutton fresh, not dried in the wind for several months.

The puffins, and their various relatives, are of great importance to the Faroese. They make the islands an ornithologist's paradise, but to the Faroese they are an important means of overcoming the islands' agricultural limitations. The countless sea-birds that visit the rocky cliffs in summer-time and (in some cases) all the year round are an endless source of food. That small and engaging bird the puffin is far the most useful of all the birds: about half-a-million of them are taken annually, to provide fresh meat for the summer and to be salted or dried for winter use. Guillemots, fulmars, gannets and other birds are taken in small quantities.

Fowling is a major island occupation, less seasonal than it was in the past. The chief tool is the *fleyg*, a large triangular net on a ten-foot pole. Since the great colonies of sea-birds are mostly found on high cliffs and crags, successful use of the *fleyg* calls for great skill and agility in dangerous circumstances. As well as a major source of food, this exercise is for the Faroese both a tradition and an exacting outdoor sport. By most standards another method of fowling – the extraction from their burrows of puffins, and of the young of the Manx shearwater by means of a long hooked stick—has a definitely unsporting character. Sport is an excellent thing, but survival comes first; and survival, in the Faroes, has never been easy.

The islanders are mostly Lutheran by religion, with some Baptists and a unit of the Salvation Army. There is also a Roman Catholic church and convent at Torshávn. The Lutheran pastor, or *prestúr*, is always on the move, visiting his scattered flock by boat, and reaching the 89

Guillemots and puffins are caught with a *fleyg* – a net on a long pole – which is reputed to have been used since Viking days.

more remote settlements only when a wedding or a christening is in prospect. He will then work briskly, performing perhaps a couple of christenings and a double wedding within an hour and a half, while the boat waits.

A Faroese wedding is a festive, stylish affair, and various interesting observances are still associated with the courtship that precedes it. Traditionally the young girls of the islands used to study the omens, using eggs and birds and flowers and herbs to ascertain and even determine their marital future. Courtship itself was a test of manhood, and in the tough circumstances of Faroese life, may have contributed to the strength of the race. The suitor might have to row a long distance over difficult waters, or leap across a deep chasm before witnesses. Even so, he might be rejected if, on entering the girl's house, he was given a three-legged stool to sit upon. In the old days, the stool used to communicate this bad news was then burnt by the girl and her friends.

When a bride eventually comes to church in the traditional dress of the islands, or in a silk gown and lace veil, she will have an elegance that one might not have expected in such a bare, remote corner of the earth. The ceremony will be over quickly, and when she leaves the church with her husband, it is probable that several young men will leap forth and surround the happy pair and fire shot-guns repeatedly into the air. Before there

were guns, inflated sheep's bladders would be beaten instead, loudly and insistently. This is an old and widespread custom, possibly to frighten off evil spirits. The practice is now regarded as a form of salute to the married couple.

After the ceremony it is usual for a man to go around the village with a bottle and glass so that everybody can toast the happy pair. But the real festivities take place the following day. A long, lavish feast begins around noon and continues, with several sittings, until about seven. Afterwards there is a crowded festive dance. The dancing is cheerful and energetic, accompanied by music that seems tuneless, but nonetheless exciting, to foreign ears. With huge enjoyment, but without drunkenness or rowdy behavior, it will probably continue until morning. Other important occasions are celebrated in much the same way – national festivals for example, or a successful whale-hunt; and the dance is accompanied not only by music and mime, but also by the recitation or chanting of long folk-poems, remembered from ancient times and only recently written down, and which celebrate the heroic past of the Vikings or the Danes or the Faroese themselves. When these festivities take place at a wedding, they are sometimes regarded as providing the real fact and validity of the marriage. The religious and official part played by the *prestur* is taken much less

A day's haul of eggs may be more than 200 – but the nine day egg-catching season allows each bird to produce another egg undisturbed.

seriously by the Faroese.

When a baby comes, his christening will, like his parents' wedding, have to be delayed until the *prestúr's* next visit. During this time his name, usually from the Bible or from the ancient sagas, will be kept secret from everybody and only revealed at the last minute. If he has to be taken a long way to the church, it is traditional for him to be wrapped up in a distinctive way and carried rapidly on the back of the strongest and most active man available: thus his own strength is fostered.

A burial is called *gravaferd*, an earth-going. Good Faroese, like good Christians elsewhere, were buried facing the east, the direction from which Christ will arise on Judgment Day. People considered bad or un-Christian were buried facing the west, and doubtful cases used to be excluded from the churchyard altogether: the bodies of shipwrecked sailors, for example, being of indeterminate religion, used to be buried where they were found.

The Trinity was always remembered in funeral rites. The body would be carried round the church three times; if it had to be taken home from the hospital at Torshávn, it would be collected in a boat which would circle three times in the harbor, while a hymn was sung, before going off to the home village for burial.

Many other aspects of Faroese life reflect these islands' long isolation from the rest of the world. For centuries their chief outside contacts were with bands of marauding pirates. History largely passed them by. Until recently they constituted a living museum of the dignified, cheerful hardihood of an old Nordic folk-culture.

Now things are changing rapidly. There is electricity in all the villages, and cars on the roads. Package-tour holiday-makers arrive at the small airport on the island of Vagár. Imported flour renders the old and picturesque vertical-shaft water-mills superfluous. Young men are attracted into public works and not into the economically crucial fishing industry. Young women leave for the easier life of Denmark, in such quantities that they seriously endanger the islands' future population. The 20th century is moving in.

The islands have become more comfortable, at the cost of losing their self-sufficiency. For long centuries these hardy people looked after themselves, with no help from outside, in an economy and a life-style that were 'primitive' in one sense, but deeply 'civilized' in another, and possibly more important, sense. The islands cannot independently support a 20th century economy and life-style. Resentment for their dependence on subsidy from Denmark may lie behind the pressures for total independence that are noticeable within the complex political structures of the Faroes. But it is not clear how any real independence could be compatible with a continued modernization and development. Perhaps the Faroese will return to the simpler ways, the isolation and the self-sufficiency of old.

Once the guillemots and puffins have been trapped by the *fleyg*, the islander wrings their necks and secures them under his belt.

Shetland Islanders
North-east Atlantic

Descended from Scots, Picts, and Norse, Shetlanders yearly celebrate a pagan festival. Their islands lie as far north as southern Greenland.

ST. MAGNUS
BAY

UNST

YELL

FETLAR

WHALSAY

SHETLAND ISLANDS

BRESSAY

FOULA

Lerwick
Scalloway

WEST
BURRA

Grutness

SCALE
0   10   20   30 km
0   10   20 Miles

FAIR ISLE

In the streets and shops of Lerwick, the capital of Britain's most remote and northerly county, the Shetland Islands, they use words like 'peerie' for 'small' and 'muckle' for 'big' and they say 'du' and 'dee' for the two cases of the word 'you'. The Shetland dialect is full of Norse words, intermingled with Scots words and set in a groundmass of English.

In Shetland, Stone Age men built their oval houses, temples and chambered burial cairns; Bronze Age people 93

A poster announces to men (or 'guizers') the coming of the yearly Up-Helly-A festival to commemorate the expulsion of the Vikings.

These cloaked celebrant Shetlanders are usually more concerned with sheep farms, fishing, or making their world-famous knitwear.

(Bottom) On the last Tuesday of January, Shetland schoolchildren out-dress their parents for the Up-Helly-A festival.

settled at Jarlshof: Iron Age men built their mysterious circular towers or *brochs* – over 40 feet high, 60 feet in diameter and the highest development of dry stone building in Europe; and Celtic missionaries from the 6th century onwards spread the Christian faith and left their sculptured shrines. But all earlier cultures were swamped by the arrival of Norse settlers in the 9th century, and their influence continued – and continues still – long after 1469 when the islands were handed over to Scotland. The Shetland surnames of Halcrow, Inkster and Gear are Norse; so are many which end in the suffix -son. But to hear the Shetland dialect spoken at its best one must go to sea on a fishing vessel or visit the country districts. The seats of a small boat are called 'tafts', the floorboards are called 'tilfers.' Many beautiful old descriptive words are used to discuss the weather. A light harmless snow shower in light wind is called a 'fluckra', but a blizzard, known as a 'blind moorie' may block the 'rodds' (roads), while 'yowes' (ewes) lie buried in 'fanns' (snowdrifts) for days afterwards.

The Norsemen handed down a way of life into which later Scottish immigrants were absorbed which continued virtually unchanged until the early 20th century and persists in Shetland today.

Traditional Shetland life was based on the croft, a few acres of green arable land between the rocky seashore and the gray heather-covered wastes on the hills. The stone-walled houses were clustered together in crofting townships, separated from neighboring settlements by several miles of moorland. Conditions were difficult but by utilizing everything possible the people could make a living. The fields produced oats, barley and (after 1730) potatoes; the hills supplied peat for fuel and pasture for flocks of small Shetland sheep whose wool was spun and knitted by the women into clothes for their families; the beaches provided seaweed for manure and shellfish as an additional source of food. But all these products combined were insufficient to maintain life. Fortunately the sea around Shetland has long been recognized as among the richest in Europe and Shetland men for generations have regarded the sea as their most important source of income.

In small open boats with a raked stem and stern, just like their forerunners, the Viking longships, the men of Shetland rowed or sailed 30 and 40 miles from land to set their lines for ling, cod and tusk. In these boats they acquired their skills in seamanship and earned their reputation as the finest seamen in the world.

The 19th century was an unhappy time for the people of Shetland. The population was divided into the mass of crofter-fishermen and a few dozen landowners or lairds with far too great a control over the lives of their tenants. The laird usually owned the crofter's house, land and fishing vessel and was also merchant for the whole district. He sold all the crofter's household requirements and bought, at below market prices, his catch of

95

(Over page) Shetlanders pose as the Viking foe of a millennium ago. Their speech abounds with Norse words — especially in sailor's talk.

In the only Shetland town of
Lerwick, jovial 'guizers',
waving eight hundred torches,
watch the blaze of 'the
last Viking longship'

fish, the knitwear produced by his wife and surplus agricultural products. If a crofter objected he could be turned out of his home.

Then in the mid 19th century the lairds discovered that grazing sheep was more profitable than crofting. So began the period of evictions when families were compelled to leave their crofts. Many young men joined the Merchant Navy but thousands emigrated to start a new life in the USA, Canada, Australia or New Zealand. The ruins of abandoned croft houses still scar the Shetland countryside. Where once was heard the laughter of children at play the wind now whistles through gaping windows, starlings nest in the ruined gables and only sheep shelter from winter storms.

The population dropped from 31,000 in 1871 to 27,000 in 1911. Then came two world wars and thousands of Shetlanders served in the forces. After World War I Shetland mourned over 600 dead; after World War II more than 300, in each case a greater proportionate loss than that of any other county in Britain. By 1961 the population was under 18,000 and as the people, the life-blood of the islands, drained away, it seemed that Shetland was dying.

In the 1960s there was a remarkable transformation. The islanders began to realize the potential of their three long neglected basic industries. It is in the fishing

industry – for herrings in summer and haddock, whiting, cod, plaice and skate that there have been the greatest developments. The Shetland fleet now includes 75 large vessels between 40 and 90 feet long manned by 450 full-time fishermen. There are also several score smaller vessels fishing part-time for lobsters, crabs and scallops. The islands of Whalsay and Burra have the largest fleets but there are important fishing communities at Lerwick, Scalloway and Ollaberry on the mainland of Shetland and also on the islands of Yell and Out Skerries. The value of the Shetland catch in 1971 was a record ($4½ million).

A modern fishing vessel is a marvel of science and technology. Her wheel-house is crammed with devices like radio to enable the skipper to keep in touch with other vessels, radar navigator to let him know his exact position and to locate other ships during fog, and echo-sounders to find out the depth of water, the nature of the seabed and the presence of shoals of fish. A modern 80-foot trawler may cost $170,000 or more. But fishing is nonetheless still a hard life – fishermen often work as much as 100 hours a week – and the returns are uncertain. In poor weeks no fish means no pay. Then come the winter storms which send boats racing for shelter and suspend fishing operations for weeks at a time.

And since World War II, and particularly since 1960, the market for the world-famous Shetland knitwear has developed so rapidly that hand knitters cannot cope with the demand. Nowadays most knitting is done on small machines and although some merchants have set up knitwear units where knitters work under factory conditions, the industry is still basically home-based with all members of the family working in their spare time to earn extra income for the family. They knit mainly plain jumpers and cardigans, sometimes with a patterned yoke evolved in isolated Fair Isle. The island women show their amazing skill particularly in the intricate designs of Fair Isle patterns and the delicate lace shawls they make in the island of Unst.

Crofting, although it survives, is now less important with the development of the other two industries. However natural, wholesome, almost idyllic is the croft by the sea with a milking cow in the byre, a few sheep on the hill and a little boat drawn up on the beach, it cannot support a family at today's standards. The produce of the croft is still a valuable addition to the family income, but the stable which once housed a work horse may now be a garage for the crofter's car which takes him daily to his job in a fish factory or knitwear unit.

When one considers the events which followed the introduction of sheep farming to Shetland a century ago it is perhaps ironic that sheep rearing should be so important to the crofter today. The islands support over 200,000 sheep and every year 40,000 lambs are shipped south to markets in Scotland. Government grants enabled crofters to enclose their shares of hill and moorland by fences, drain their land, plow it and re-seed it. Over thousands of acres where once only heather bloomed in the autumn and white tufts of wild cotton grass waved in the wind, now fat sheep stand grazing among grass and clover.

The croft houses are now new or rebuilt. Electric lighting has replaced the old paraffin lamps. The introduction of deep freeze units has virtually ended the need to salt meat and fish as a standby for winter. No longer are oats and barley ground in little water mills – it is more convenient to buy flour in 3 lb bags at the local shop. As the islands are far from self-supporting, a wide range of goods is imported by the twice-weekly passenger and cargo vessel *St Clair* from Aberdeen.

But still here and there old customs continue. Although coal and oil have largely replaced peat as fuel, in every district there are men who prepare a section of moorland for peat cutting, and using a tushkar, the old Shetland peat spade, dig out the wet slabs of shiny black peat, building them carefully into a 'wall' for the first stage of drying.

In 1971 oil was discovered east of Shetland and exploration was extended to the sea-bed all around the islands. A new race of technicians arrived with business men in their wake, to guarantee their share of the expected boom. It is certain that the decade following the oil gush of 1972 will see more changes than in any other in Shetland's long history.

About a third of Shetland's population lives in Lerwick. It is the only town in Shetland and the administrative and commercial center for a population of over 17,000. At times the flags of a dozen nations fly from the mastheads of ships in the harbor, for Lerwick also dominates a wide area of the North Sea. The old part of the town has the greatest attraction for visitors. In the south, the old houses bathe their feet in the sea and tiny private jetties are a reminder of the days when smuggling played a great part in the trade of Lerwick. Streets are paved wall to wall, and are as twisting as the old shore-line which they follow, over the steep contours of the town.

The Shetlanders do not welcome the prospect of a transformation. They already have a prosperous economy and ample amusements in which they blend the modern with the traditional. They have public halls and community centers in which they hold dances, whist drives and concerts; they play football and hockey and each district holds, as the biggest event of the year, a yachting regatta. They dance local variations of the Scottish reel, and the old-fashioned Foula reel and the Shetland reel. An ancient dance survives in the Papa Stour sword dance: its tune has unmistakeable Scandinavian characteristics. Shetland's musical heritage is mainly of fiddle tunes, a few of which have words set to them. The tunes fall into three main groups: wedding tunes, 'trowie' tunes – said to have been learned near the haunts or trows or fairies – and reel tunes. Fiddle music has recently been revived. A group of musicians, who call themselves 'the forty fiddlers' entertain important visitors.

Greater importance is attached to Christmas in Shetland than in other parts of Scotland, but this does not detract from the importance of the New Year celebrations. As an excuse to prolong the festivities, some districts still hold additional celebrations 11 days later to mark the festivals according to the old Julian calendar which was abandoned in 1752.

The greatest spectacle of all is the festival of Up-Helly-A at Lerwick, the capital, on the night of the last Tuesday of January. The flames from up to 800 torches carried by squads of 'guizers' in ancient Viking dress illuminate the crowds lining the streets. At the head of the procession a Norse galley is dragged to its burning place in the center of the town. The burning of the galley marks the end of only the first part of the proceedings. Then begins the round of the halls which each of 50 or so squads must visit in strict order. Here the night's revelry is held, organized by hard-working hostesses. The festival of Up-Helly-A can be traced back to the pagan festival with which the Norsemen ended their long mid-winter celebration of Yule. It was their way of welcoming back the sun after the long dark nights of mid-winter.

Canary Islanders and their Guanche forbears

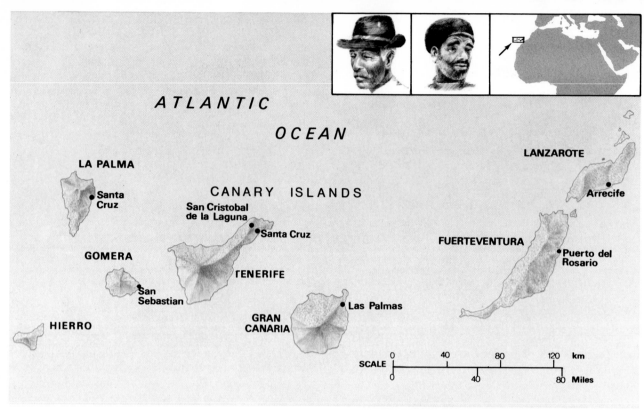

ATLANTIC

OCEAN

CANARY ISLANDS

LA PALMA
• Santa Cruz

San Cristobal de la Laguna
• Santa Cruz

GOMERA

TENERIFE

• San Sebastian

HIERRO

GRAN CANARIA
• Las Palmas

LANZAROTE
• Arrecife

FUERTEVENTURA
• Puerto del Rosario

SCALE

| 0 | 40 | 80 | 120 | km |

| 0 | | 40 | | 80 | Miles |

Around 82 BC the Roman Republic conducted a campaign against one of its own citizens, Quintus Sertorius. He had been exiled to Spain, and had founded there a 'new Rome' as a kind of ideological challenge to the old Rome. The challenge was taken and Quintus Sertorius found himself on the run. The time came when his fleet touched in at Huelva in Spain.

There, the Greek historian Plutarch tells us, Sertorius met sailors recently returned from the Canary Islands. 'These are two in number, separated from each other by a narrow channel, and lying at the distance of ten thousand furlongs from the African coast. They are called "the Fortunate Islands." Rain seldom falls there, and then falls moderately; while they have usually soft breezes, which scatter such rich dews, that the soil is not only good for sowing and planting, but spontaneously produces the most excellent fruits, and those in such abundance, that the inhabitants have only to indulge themselves in the enjoyment of ease and leisure. The air is always pleasant and salubrious, through the happy temperature of the seasons, and their insensible transition into each other. For the north and the east winds, which blow from our continent, are dissipated and lost in the immense interval; and the sea winds (that is, the south and the west) bring with them from the ocean slight and gentle showers, but still more frequently only a refreshing moisture, which imperceptibly scatters plenty over their plains. Hence it is generally believed, even among the barbarians, that these are the Elysian Fields and the seats of the blessed, which Homer has described in all the charms of verse.'

The Canary Islands are actually seven in number, but otherwise the description is just about exact. It appealed strongly to Sertorius, and he longed to turn away from politics and war and settle in those happy islands just as in our own time countless people chiefly from northern Europe, have felt the same attraction and have come to holiday or even to settle in those fortunate islands.

They are particularly fortunate in lying off the beaten track. The Canary Islands are in the Atlantic Ocean 60 to 70 miles off the coast of south-west Morocco. Plutarch's ten thousand furlongs are a romantic exaggeration. They were known in ancient times and were possibly visited by the ancient Phoenicians and, around 1400 BC, by Sesostris, King of Egypt. But until the great explorations began in the 15th century, they lay off the busy commercial shipping routes and history passed them by.

The islands were conquered first by French and then by Spanish invaders between 1402 and 1496. Since then, they have had some involvement in history. Columbus used them as a base. They were a center of the slave trade. In 1797, Nelson lost his right arm and sustained his only reverse at Santa Cruz de Tenerife. More recently the

The arid lunar landscape of
the eastern Canaries
contrasts with the greener
isles to the west, where 'soft
breezes scatter rich dews'

A majority of *Canarios* are Catholic. From a pulpit on Lanzarote, a student explains the catechism to his fellow students.

(Bottom) It is not uncommon to see camels used for farm work in the Canaries, for they lie only 67 miles off the Moroccan coast.

islands have been prominent as a base and port of call for shipping, especially for cruise liners. Las Palmas, on the island of Gran Canaria, is now Spain's busiest port. Since the 1950s a tourist boom has radically altered the islands' economy and character.

Before the 15th century, the indigenous inhabitants had long lived not only in almost complete isolation from the rest of the world but also in isolation from one another since they had no boats. They were also isolated from their own past as they had no writing. So in the Canary Islands, there survived until recent times a people and a culture that can loosely be called 'prehistoric.' The people the Spaniards conquered with some difficulty were Paleolithic men. They lived in caves and used stone implements. Only by their skill in pottery might they be called Neolithic. Then, rapidly, they were hustled from their Stone Age life into the Iron Age and the more or less modern world, with no Bronze Age in between.

These ancient people are usually called the Guanches although this name should more properly be reserved for the aboriginal inhabitants of Tenerife and the other western islands. It is a contraction of *Guanchenerfe*, from *quan* ('a son') and *Chenerfe*, the name of Tenerife, so strictly the Guanches are the sons of that island. In practice the term is used more loosely.

Our knowledge of the Guanches is fragmentary, for to those 15th century Spanish adventurers the Guanches were enemies to be defeated, slaves to be sold, pagans to be baptised, and notably beautiful women to be married. Anthropological research and observation were not what the Spaniards had chiefly in mind, even before the conquest was completed. The process of inter-marriage and interbreeding had begun. For a long time now, the Guanches have ceased to exist as a separate people for they have been completely assimilated by centuries of Spanish colonists. Culturally, the islands are almost completely Spanish. But certain customs of the Guanches still survive, the islands are full of their relics and remains, and the observant visitor today will often notice the survival of their distinct physical types.

Their origin is mysterious. In spite of the occasional visits of outsiders from ancient times the 'Fortunate Islands' were thought of in mythological terms as the lands of the blessed, where a dragon guarded the gardens of the Hesperides. The actual story of the indigenous people, and of their arrival at the islands, was recorded neither by the outside world nor by the Guanches themselves. Only a few riddling sentences remain of their ancient language. Romantic speculation about their origin and the ancient history of their island was inevitable.

The most intriguing theory is that the Canary Islands are the last remaining fragments of the continent of Atlantis, which according to Plato once stood where the Atlantic Ocean is now, but sank, leaving these few islands and these few remnants of its people. This theory

is contradicted by recent research indicating that the Aegean island of Thera – part of today's Santorin – was the site of Atlantis.

According to another old report, the Guanches are descended from an African tribe exiled for defying Roman authority. Before being sent off to the islands, these people had their tongues cut out to prevent them boasting of their defiance.

There may be truth in this story, but it is unlikely to be the whole truth. On the other hand, it does account for their lack of oral tradition and it does tie in with the remarkable practice, which still survives on the islands of Gomera and Hierro, of communicating by means of a highly-articulated kind of whistling. 'The natives' said an early French visitor 'speak the most remarkable of all the languages of these islands, talking with their lips as if they had no tongues.' And the present-day visitor can find them still doing it as a matter of course, sending long and precise messages over distances of a mile or more by a piercing whistle, the tone and the length of note varying according to meaning, the whole code being ultimately based (in contradiction of the legend) upon the Spanish language.

It would be tempting, but almost certainly misleading, to see in this practice a confirmation of that story of the tongueless exiles. Much more probably, it was developed as the Swiss developed their yodelling, as a practical means of communication across ravines and between craggy mountain-sides.

It would be equally rash to accept the story that the Guanches were of Egyptian origin, since they practised the art of mummifying their dead. This was in fact their most highly-developed art, and Egyptian influence may have been involved, especially if Homer's story of an Egyptian visit is true.

But the Guanches themselves appear to have been a fairly pure remnant of the old European Cro-Magnon stock who displaced the earlier Neanderthal inhabitants and were themselves displaced, though not exterminated, by other peoples who came later on from the east. From this stock, with much later admixture, come the Basques and the Celts, the Berbers and the Iberian peoples. When the conquering Spaniards began to intermarry with the Guanches, there was already a distant affinity of blood.

In the Canary Islands today we can identify, partly by cranial measurement, the Cro-Magnon type in about one third of all the people and in nearly half the people of Gomera, as well as in all the pre-conquest mummies and skeletons. In the western islands especially – in Gomera, Hierro, La Palma, Tenerife, and even in Gran Canaria – the visitor will notice the distinguishing marks of the true Guanche, in the tall stature of certain individuals, in their light hair and brilliant blue eyes. The aboriginal type which predominates in the eastern islands is by contrast brown-eyed, shorter and considerably darker skinned than any peninsular Spaniard.

In the hard light of the noonday sun a Lanzarote family returns home from the fields for lunch and a siesta in the Spanish tradition.

(Top) Guanches – the mysterious first inhabitants – now exist only as mummies, and in the blood of the Spanish invaders with whom they mixed.

ATLANTIC Canary Islanders

Since the 1950's a tourist
boom has hit the Canaries.
Here a caravan of visitors
ascends the 'Mountain of Fire'
— Lanzarote's volcano.

04

Two Lanzarote *canarios* extract salt from the sea around their islands — in salt pans where the water evaporates.

Our knowledge of the life and society of the Guanches is based upon archaeological study of their relics and remains and upon the accounts of them written by the 15th century Spanish invaders. These are often interesting but written well after the conquest, when the assimilation process was well advanced, and not necessarily reliable. Even the earliest reports may be romanticized. Soon the European mind was taken up with the idea of the 'noble savage' – the idea that primitive peoples who lived untouched by the corrupting hand of civilization in remote places might be expected to retain a certain primal innocence, a noble unspoilt simplicity of character and conduct.

Thus the Garden of Eden might be found again, or what the ancients called 'the reign of Saturn.' This idea is reflected in Shakespeare's *Tempest*, and it recurs constantly in the early accounts of the American Indians; it may be partly responsible for the somewhat idyllic terms in which the society of the Guanches – despite its heathen character – is described by most of the early writers. According to one account they were virtuous, honest, and brave, and the finest qualities of humanity were found united in them: magnanimity, skill, courage, athletic prowess, strength of soul and body, pride of character, nobleness of demeanor, a smiling physiognomy, an intelligent and patriotic devotedness.

This may be an idealized picture; but the Guanches do seem to have displayed a number of admirable human qualities, perhaps reflected nowadays in the gentle, good-humored atmosphere which adds so much to the holiday-maker's enjoyment. The Guanches appear to have shown mercy and mildness towards their aggressive and sometimes treacherous invaders. They preferred not to kill Spanish prisoners but rather to make them work as servants, especially in the despised trade of butchering. Sometimes they released them and on at least one occasion took some trouble and risk to get them back to their comrades on their ships.

Guanche religion varied from one island to another. On Tenerife, they seemed to have a clear idea of a God who lived on the summit of Pico de Tiede – the 3,707 foot mountain in the center of the island – and of a devil or Satan who lived in underground fires below it. Elsewhere there were varied kinds of paganism; the Spanish priests complained that the Guanches knew nothing of immortality, of death, nor of future punishment.

Catholic disapproval of Guanche paganism was tempered, however, by the remarkable fact that long before the Spanish conquerors and missionaries arrived, Tenerife appeared to have been privileged by a visitation of the Blessed Virgin. Late in the 14th century, it is said, two Guanche herdsmen found a statue of the Virgin and Child standing on a rock by the sea. Knowing nothing of Christianity, they at once recognized the sacred character of this image, especially as one of them threw

These wrestlers look Spanish, yet some inhabitants on the western islands have fair hair and blue eyes — traces of Guanche ancestry.

107

For the unmarried girls of
La Orotava, on Tenerife, the
Corpus Christi festival is an
occasion for dressing up and
— perhaps — meeting suitors.

On Gomera, a whistled language survives. Legend has it that Guanche rebels against Rome were cast away with their tongues cut out.

a stone at it and was punished by immediate paralysis. The kings, or *menceys*, of Tenerife considered the matter, and it was decided to enshrine and worship this statue in a cave: pagans still, the Guanches now had a cult comparable to that of Lourdes or Fatima.

When the Spaniards came, they were astonished at this mark of heavenly favor: from the beauty of the statue, said to excel anything they had seen before, they concluded that it was of supernatural origin. At one point, it was seized and carried off to the eastern island of Fuerteventura. But it responded by turning its face to the wall, and when a plague broke out as well, these hints were accepted and the statue was returned to Tenerife. There a basilica was built early in the 16th century to house and honor it. In 1826 a freak storm brought a tidal wave which carried the Virgin of Candelaria out to the sea from which she had come.

So runs the story. The statue the Canary Islanders now venerate is an admitted copy and resembles many 14th-century works of the Christian Mediterranean.

In the religious life of the old Guanches, there were other foreshadowings of their Christian future. For one thing, they had a custom that resembled baptism so closely that it suggested some long-forgotten Christian influence. A woman, specially chosen like a god-mother, would pour water over the head of a new-born baby. Then they appear to have had clerical or monastic communities of both men and women. A cynic might also comment that their priests, who came from the noble class, resembled certain priests elsewhere in their ingenious theological justifications of the class system and the status quo. The Guanche nobles, the priests used to explain, had been created first, and given flocks to feed them; later on, the common people were created in quantity, but with fewer flocks or none. They were to serve the nobles, who would feed them by their bounty.

The Guanches had kings as well as nobles. Kingship varied from place to place in the islands and included both hereditary and elective elements. In Tenerife, after the death of a king who ruled the whole island, inheritance was divided among his nine sons, who became the *menceys*. Later at the election of a new *mencey* with grand ceremony, oaths were given and taken and blessed by banquets and games. The islanders would apparently even then honor the new *mencey* and gain his compassion for their families by ritual suicide: one or two people would celebrate the *mencey's* elevation by throwing themselves over a cliff.

Guanche society was a flock-owning aristocracy and a distinct peasantry. They kept sheep, goats, pigs and rabbits for food. Grazing land was carefully shared, but was frequently the cause of disputes and wars. There were no metallic arts or implements. Cultivation, which was women's work, was done with tools of obsidian (volcanic glass), wood, and bone. The land was neither irrigated nor manured and soon became exhausted. Then people simply moved on and broke new ground, as some African peoples still do. They did some fishing: one method, still in use, involves poisoning the fish with a substance from the euphorbia plant which stupefies the fish and brings them to the surface for easy taking.

The Guanches' staple food, as of the poorer *Canarios* today, was a kind of paste or dough called *gofio*, made from toasted and salted grain, ground in a small hand-mill and mixed with water or goat's milk or fat. Meat and fish were not abundant. Their diet was so simple that one Spanish chronicler expressed his astonishment that men so valiant, with such strength and agility and with such fine faculties as they possessed, should have been brought up on such rough, coarse food.

The Guanches' strength and agility and their fine physique and good teeth, were widely remarked upon by the conquerors. They are described as lightly built, great runners and jumpers, 'for they are accustomed to the crags of this mountainous island. They leap from rock to rock, bare-footed, like goats, and clear jumps of incredible width. They throw stones accurately and powerfully, so that they can hit whatever they wish. They have such strong arms that with a few blows they

Fish is part of the *Canarios'* staple food: on Tenerife, villagers pick cod off the racks where it is dried in the sun.

(Bottom) Volcanic soil is infertile, but retains all moisture. From Roman times, Lanzarote has been famous for its grapes.

can shatter a shield in pieces.' A heavy stone, said to have been used as a trial of strength in Guanche times, is still preserved at Arico in Tenerife. The record says that it was often raised to shoulder-height, presumably by one man: no single man can even move it now. The Guanches' favorite sport was wrestling.

One can see why the Spaniards found them so hard to capture alive and harder still to conquer. They were a tough, defined people. Although they were so fully and quickly assimilated, they have left their mark upon the islands. Although politically two Spanish provinces, the islands are distinct and different from Spain. The Spanish language is spoken throughout the islands, though in a dialect, and the customs and way of life are mostly characteristically Spanish. But there is a strong sense of separate identity and local patriotism, even between one island and another, and some resentment of the distant rule of Madrid. The people are *Canarios* and prefer to be so described: to call them *Españoles* is to insult them.

The modern visitor will notice the contrast between the mountainous islands to the west and the flat, arid, lunar landscape of Lanzarote and Fuerteventura to the east. Remembering what Plutarch said about the dews of these islands of low rainfall, he will note the ingenuity with

The Romans called the Canaries 'the Fortunate Islands' for even then they were famed for a temperate climate and gentle sea breeze.

The stage is set for La Orotava's festival of Corpus Christi, colored by ancient Guanche religions which curiously paralleled Christianity.

In island costume this man plays the *pilot de agua* at the carnival. Only one other person knows how to play the ancient instrument.

which the dry volcanic dust is used in those eastern islands to provide moisture for the vines and other crops. It does nothing to nourish the plants, but it does attract and hold the heavy dew.

The islands are more prosperous than they were before the great tourist boom of the 1950s, but still poor by European standards. Fish and sweet potatoes and yams and some meat supplement *gofio*, the staple food. There are good schools, and a university was founded in 1701, but communication is difficult, many villages are isolated and literacy is far from universal. In many remote communities, the only person who can read and write is the parish priest; for this and for other reasons, he is a great power among his people. To the isolated *Canarios* the great festivals of the Church are, with the occasional bull fight or wrestling-match, likely to seem more important than the headline events of the outside world.

Only in the remote villages, and on the small, isolated island of Hierro, are the traditional costumes still worn: the *Canarios* mostly wear the normal European dress. A few, however, still follow the practise of their Guanche ancestors and live in caves. This is not always in squalor and poverty: the visitor who ventures into the highlands will sometimes find a complete village where every house and even the church is an elaborate cave, hewn from the easily-worked volcanic rock and fitted with doors and windows, cool in summer and warm in winter, and extremely clean and comfortable.

Today bananas and, on a smaller scale, tomatoes are the chief cash crops. The enormous cochineal industry of the 19th century, ruined by the introduction of synthetic dyestuffs, has nevertheless left its mark upon the islands: the nopal cactus, specially introduced to feed the cochineal insects, has flourished so abundantly that it now seems an essential and characteristic part of the Canary landscape.

It is a landscape which tends to charm the visitor, despite the Saharan aridity of the eastern islands. With the continuously pleasant climate and the peacefulness of life, the islands live up to their ancient title and can certainly be considered fortunate. Nature or the Creator must take one part of the credit for this, and the tradition and culture of Spain must take another part — but these Gardens of the Hesperides would not be what they are now if it were not for those 'noble savages' the Guanches, the last surviving prehistoric men of Europe.

Strangers to the Canaries
are never told the symbolism
of these faceless women who,
at festivals, appear veiled,
draped and gloved.

Tristan da Cunha Islanders
South Atlantic

Tristans depend on boating prowess. Without a natural harbor, they can be 'nighted' at sea for five days on end in foul weather.

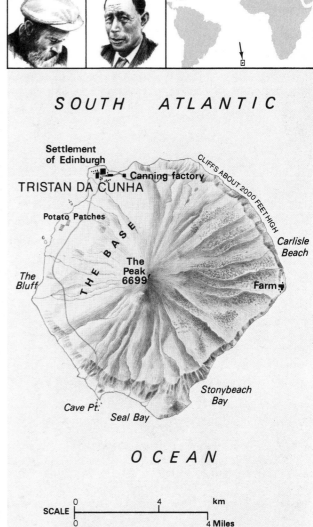

SOUTH ATLANTIC

Settlement
of Edinburgh
TRISTAN DA CUNHA
Canning factory
CLIFFS ABOUT 2000 FEET HIGH
Potato Patches
THE BASE
The
Peak
6699
Carlisle
Beach
The
Bluff
Farm
Stonybeach
Bay
Cave Pt.
Seal Bay

OCEAN

SCALE 0 — 4 — km
        0 — 4 Miles

The 260 men, women and children of Tristan da Cunha are the world's loneliest islanders. A round volcanic mountain seven miles wide, Tristan squats in the middle of the south Atlantic Ocean roughly halfway between Rio de Janeiro (2,100 miles to the west) and Cape Town (1,700 miles southeast). The islanders' nearest neighbors live 1,200 miles off to the north on the island of St Helena, where Napoleon spent his last days. Twenty-five miles off Tristan there are the tiny islands of Nightlingale and Inaccessible but no one lives on them except the birds.

Tristan is shaped like a wheel spoked by numerous precipitous gulches that radiate out and down from the central mountain crater almost 7,000 feet above the sea. As avalanches of cindery rock often hurtle down the gulches, once boiling floes of lava, they are too

'Keep it on the island!'
shout footballers. All 300
Tristans live here in
Edinburgh, known simply to
them as 'the settlement'.

A British salvage party
inspects damage after the
1961 eruption. Tristans were
evacuated – but in two years
most had come back.

Early every morning outside
the village hall the
British Administrator
watches the Union Jack
being hoisted.

dangerous to climb. Even more capricious than the land is the sea that surrounds Tristan. Storms suddenly burst from nowhere. And on Tristan there is no hiding from them as they sweep right round the island and rampage up every gulley. As the islanders say, 'There's no lee on Tristan.' The waters themselves abound with sharks, and in the old days with killer whales too. The dark cindery beaches give no protection to incoming ships. Even when the sea is calm, landing is tricky. For hundreds of years the only people who came ashore were shipwreck survivors.

There is little to describe on the dry land apart from the mountain itself and the occasional precarious shelf where cattle and sheep can graze. There is only one place where houses can be built – the tongue of land near the shore where 'the settlement' is sited. There is no wood except 'the island tree,' a type of buckwood that is no good for building and burns too fast for firemaking. The soil is scarce and poor; crops often die of disease. The only friendly aspect of Tristan's nature – so they said – was the long-extinct volcano that would never erupt again. But even the volcano turned nasty – in August 1961 it violently erupted. After struggling for 150 years with the three elements water, earth and air, the fourth, fire, overwhelmed the islanders. Earthquakes that preceded the eruption jammed doors tight and cracked walls. The ground heaved, split open and rose in a bubble as the volcano looked for a vent. Finally it exploded not far from the settlement forcing the inhabitants off the island. They were evacuated; the authorities in England assumed it was for good.

Yet to the surprise of many, almost all went back in 1963. In fact until 1810 no one did live there. A Portuguese admiral first spotted the place in 1608 and gave it his name. But as a stopping-place Tristan gave no promise, for there is nowhere to land. In 1810 an American pirate named Lambert decided to defy nature and make a stand on the island. He hoisted his own flag. The toy king was joined by two other renegades, but three years later only one of the trio was left – Tomaso Currie, a Genoese Irishman who probably murdered his two companions. With Napoleon exiled to neighboring St Helena in 1815, 'Italian Tom' was joined by a detachment of British soldiers sent to Tristan under a young South African captain banished for duelling.

When they left five months later, Scottish-born Corporal William Glass volunteered to stay on with his teenage Cape-colored wife and their two small children. Glass, tough, kindly and humble, is the real founder of the island people. When he died in 1853 he had ensured the community's survival; he had firmly established the tradition of equality that still goes on, and had bred 16 children whose descendants inhabit the island today.

In his first years on the island, Glass was joined by a few drop-out sailors who soon tired of their lone bachelor existence. So five women from St Helena – a fat middle-

Martha Rodgers bears one
of the islanders' seven
surnames. The first
Tristan Rodgers was a
roaming American whaler.

Even for major undertakings like building the church — which took 70 years — no-one on Tristan gives orders. Yet the system works well.

Albert Glass, descendant of the community's founder, is Tristan's first policeman. Crime was unknown before the evacuation to England.

Before the British education officer came, the Tristans' only teachers were visiting clergy, whose activities they strictly circumscribed.

aged negress and four mulattos – volunteered to settle on Tristan and marry the lonely bachelors. Sixty-six-year-old Tom Swain swore he would marry the first lady ashore – and he and the negress had a happy partnership blessed by several children. A Dutchman named Groen – soon afterwards, Green – and a couple of American whalers, Hagan and Rogers, joined the slowly growing community. At the end of the 19th century, two Genoese sailors, Lavarello and Repetto, picked Tristan for their home. Today the seven surnames – Glass, Green, Swain, Hagan, Rogers, Lavarello and Repetto – are still the only ones on the island.

It is no surprise that looks vary widely. There are gingerheads and black frizzy-haired Tristans. Complexions are generally dark, harking back to the St Helena women or the first Mrs Glass. Two Irish women who came at the turn of the century are the islanders' only other female progenitors. Inevitable inbreeding has little affected the islanders – apart from a recurring eye complaint – but marriage of close cousins is certainly discouraged.

In style of dress the Tristans are still strangely old-world, though their forced stay in England has given the youth a modern look. The women still cover their heads with the white Afrikaaner 'kappies' that the original Mrs Glass favored. And people still wear the cow-hide moccasins that Tristans have always worn.

Tristan language has always surprised outsiders. 'How you is?' asks an islander. 'I's well' comes the reply. 'We's wery loyal to Henglan' they say (though there was much they disliked when they went there in 1961). Cake means bread; bread means ship's biscuits. Wheelbarrows and oxcarts are called buses and trains. Island place-names recall past events – Down-Where-The-Minister-Land-His-Things, Jew's Point (after a shipwreck survivor), Ridge-Where-The-Goat-Jump-Off, Tommy's Eye Loose (a corruption of 'oil-house'), and so on.

Old customs are cherished. Islanders love to dance folk dances long since dead in England – Tapioca's Big Toe, Hook Legs, The Break 'Er Down Dance, all vigorously performed to fiddle and accordion. Unless formally engaged, no one may dance with the same partner more than three times. If the couple are engaged, then the youth can escort his girl home, but not otherwise. Tristans may not marry before they are 21. When the girl knits socks for the young man and adds colored rings around the tops, she has accepted him. Then she begins to do his washing too.

The houses look like Scottish crofts, presumably through the founder's influence. The walls are built of huge chunks of brown rough-hewn lava rock, fitted together like a jig-saw. Even so, some have been blown down. Each cottage is surrounded by a square patch of New Zealand flax which is used to thatch the roof. Beams and rafters and furniture are made of driftwood. An old oar marked with the name of its sunk ship is often proudly displayed. (The magnificent church bell is the relic of a wreck.) The door to the cottage opens halfway down, like a stable's. The modern flush lavatories, recently installed and known as 'flash' lavatories by the islanders, are placed outside the front door, due to an architect's quirk.

If the houses of Tristan are sturdy enough, the islanders' food supply is less reliable. Yet communication with the outer world was till recently so rare that the Tristans risked starvation unless they could manage to subsist on the scarce and meager soil. Potatoes are the staple diet. There is a strip of land above the settlement known as 'the patches.' Here the Tristans, family by family, work hard all the year round to ensure a decent crop – but rats came with a wrecked ship last century and diseases also threaten the potatoes. At the turn of the century there were 700 cows, but the islanders were ignorant of stocking and breeding and there was a sudden drastic decline in numbers. Sheep are used more for their wool than their meat. The islanders fish, and they catch birds, especially the yellow-beaked albatross which they call the 'mollymawk'. As 'molly' couples unfortunately only produce one chick a year, their numbers are dwindling. Petrels and 'pinnamins' (penguins) provide oil and fat for cooking. Apples grow on the far side of the island, but you can only get there by boat. Donkeys and pairs of bullocks pulling wood-wheeled carts lug loads to and from the settlement and the beach, but tractors and asphalt roads have recently been introduced.

At first the community survived by barter. Ships would be glad to anchor offshore for a few days while families of Tristans took turns to supply the ships with fresh meat and vegetables in return for such luxuries as flour, bread and sugar. Nails, canvass, rope and paint were all highly valued. Even rusty old nails were straightened and carefully kept. But as the sail gave way to steam and oil, Tristan became redundant as a stop-over place. Wrecks, once fairly frequent – there was usually one big one every five years or so – became rare. The islanders were well and truly on their own.

There are times, like thatching, when all islanders club together. A man who wants to make a new roof at the beginning of the year collects all his friends to help him. He in turn is expected, but not obliged, to repay his neighbors. It is friendship, not business. And there are no friends in business, say the islanders. In the same manner, women usually have plenty of helpers when they come to card the wool. On Tristan helping your neighbors is something more than a case of many hands making light work. Carding and thatching are undertaken in a festive spirit, out of the islanders' warm feeling for their community life.

Islanders are famous for their boating prowess and for the cooperative rather than authoritarian way in which the crews work together. Building the vessels themselves is a combined effort, undertaken with delicacy 11?

Islanders now profit from
the world-wide sale of their
stamps. Philatelists dream
of a complete, valuable,
Tristan collection.

(Top) A family group shows the Tristans' racial diversity: negro mixed with Irish, Dutch, Scottish, Italian and American ancestry.

and skill. Pastmasters at the art are the Lavarello family – the first Lavarello was an ingenious builder. Only the slender frames of the boat are wooden as wood is scarce. The rest of the boat is made of sealskin, canvas or even old mailbags, stretched tightly over the skeleton. The original Lavarello boat was extended as the Lavarello family expanded. The boat was almost totally rebuilt from the original basic materials as year after year their family of grown men increased, until finally it was big enough to accommodate a crew of nine. But as the boat is composed of the elements of the first boat it is affectionately regarded as the same boat. On other boats the crew usually numbers four or five.

Tristan boatmen tend to be emotionally attached to their boats. On each longboat there is no skipper, orders are rare, and quiet when they come. Without instructions and without a hierarchy each oarsman simply understands, and carries out, his job. Seamen from outside, accustomed to discipline and barked commands, are amazed at the Tristans' apparently easy mastery of the whimsical and frequently vicious seas that surround their island rock. Whether they row or sail only short distances, or across to the neighbouring islands, the Tristans seem to negotiate the waves and crashing surf without difficulty.

The most exuberant events of the year, in which almost every islander participates, are the Appling Trip when they go to collect apples from the wild orchard on the far side of the island, and the annual journey known as the Fatting in March or April. Amid great teasing and laughter, the Tristans row the 25 miles to Nightingale Island where they camp at night and catch oil-bearing petrels by day. They return after a fortnight, boats laden with oil and fat. The Fatting is like a holiday, almost a religious event. It is inconceivable to Tristans that they should ever have to forfeit it.

Since 1948 the British authorities have appointed a Resident Administrator to set up reforms and transform Tristan from a precarious subsistence economy into a cash-economy island. A crayfish canning factory has been built in which islanders work long hours for small cash rewards.

A year and a half in England did not fail to rub off on the Tristans, particularly on the young. The status symbols are the radio and the gramophone. And islanders now buy fertilizer with cash; before, they climbed the dangerous mountainside to collect cow manure. But Europe's money mentality bemused the Tristans, even if it did enable them to buy the occasional luxury. They resented working under a boss and hated the idea of contract – it seemed natural that you took a few days off to tend the potatoes or help a friend thatch. If you did not feel like work one morning, surely you just had to send your son or brother along. And nothing could put off the Fatting.

In 1969 the islanders' way of life clashed dramatically with the new British order of things when employees of the canning factory were allowed no leave to take part in the Fatting. The Tristans went on strike. Their egalitarian society made them obdurate against the hierarchy and the new regulations and restrictions clashed with the fundamentally anarchic principles of the islanders. But anarchy on Tristan never meant disorder or unruliness and the sole policeman – a recent British innovation – seems unnecessary on an island which has never seen even a case of fisticuffs in its whole history. The eighteen months the islanders spent in England following the eruption of the volcano are remembered by many as a time of 'corruption'. The violence they saw on the streets of some English towns was something they could not understand.

The authorities have at last sensed that Tristans will hold on to their egalitarian and anarchic ideals. Contracts for fish-factory workers are now flexible. The administrator holds meetings, but they are muted affairs, and hand follows cautious hand at voting time. Some of the youth will doubtless be attracted away from the island – but this has happened throughout its history. It is likely that a healthy caucus of Tristans will stay put on the island and maintain its traditions.

11

Older women carry on the tradition of carding and spinning their own wool, but younger islanders prefer imported clothing.

Falkland Islanders
South-west Atlantic

The windblown Falklands, just
north of the Roaring Forties,
lie 1,000 miles away from
Montevideo, the
nearest friendly port.

SOUTH
ATLANTIC
OCEAN

WEST
FALKLAND Hill Cove
Settlement

Douglas
Settlement

FALKLAND SOUND

Stanley

Goose
Green Pt Darwin

EAST
FALKLAND

SCALE

0   40   80   120   km

0   40   80 Miles

More than eight thousand miles of heavy Atlantic seas lie between the people of the Falkland Islands and England, their mother country. By ship those eight thousand miles may take as long as a month to cover, and even from Montevideo, 1,000 miles away, the trip out to the islands takes three and a half days. There are no shipping links between Argentinian ports and the Falklands although they are only 300 miles apart.

For Falkland islanders (or Kelpers as they call themselves, after kelp, the seaweed they collected, from whose ash iodine was extracted), contact with the outside world is not easy; it is always subject to the whim of the weather, the capricious seas, and the powerful, cold winds of the Roaring Forties which almost ceaselessly whip across the islands. The islanders become accustomed to isolation; they are familiar with its hardships. Their visits to England tend to be cursory. Newspapers from England are two months old by the time they reach the islands.

121

A small boat sets off to one of the two hundred smaller islands where a shepherd's sole company is 4,000 sheep.

A sheep station is a tiny community in itself — a 'big house', shepherds' house, wool sheds and a diesel generator for the long dark winters.

Wives of isolated farmers
spin their own wool and knit
sweaters and cardigans, as
they used to in the Scotland
of their forefathers.

The Falkland Islands seem, to the outsider, to offer few compensations for their isolation; they appear cold, unwelcoming and harsh and windblown. They have none of the extravagant colors or fauna of tropical isles, nor the grand majesty of some of the islands further south on the fringe of Antarctica. To the people of Europe and the west who inhabit the crowded metropolis and the concrete and glass skyscrapers, these things make islands exotic and attractive. Isolation also has its virtues – until the man accustomed to mass media and constant stimulation discovers he is at a loss without them. The landscape of the Falkland Islands is barren; the undulating hills rarely become mountains; there are no trees, little vegetation; the radio catches only the BBC's foreign service; the islanders are insular and their conversations confined to local matters. Falkland Island life falls far short of the sophisticated urban ideal of island bliss.

The Falkland group has two large islands (East and West Falkland) and some 200 smaller islands, many of which are uninhabited. When the first known landing was made on the islands in 1690 none were inhabited. Within the next hundred years two settlements were made, one French and one British. In 1766 the French handed over their settlement to the Spanish, whose colony lasted until 1810. This move was later to become the basis for the claim of Argentina (the inheritor of that part of the Spanish Empire) to rule the islands and the cause of the present unfriendly relations between the islands and Argentina. The British began their colonization of the islands in earnest during the early part of the 19th century. In 1892 the islands were designated a Crown Colony and became a part of the Empire which then ruled a third of the world. Among the 2,000 inhabitants of the islands today, there are people who still remember some of those early settlers. A few actually draw a proud line of descent from 30 pensioners who were brought to the islands from Chelsea Royal Hospital in 1849. The pensioners were already past the prime of life by Victorian standards, yet many were under thirty. Some found life too hard, others thought it grim. Those who could not make good returned to England, but the others stayed on as permanent colonists. In 1858 they were joined by a group of 35 marines and their families. There was plenty of work, ship-repairing and selling provisions to passing boats. By 1851 the Falkland Island Trading Company had been established and sheep farming was introduced. It brought in both new men and sheep which were to become the basis of the Falkland economy.

There is no early history of the Falkland Islands, except perhaps that geologically the islands seem to be a fragment of the African continent rather than of the South American land mass. Over millions of years the fragments drifted westward, to become the Falklands, a mere 300 miles from the coast of South America. Before the settlements of little more than 100 years ago there

A sheep station may have as
many as 50,000 sheep to shear
at shearing time. In a single
day the men may gather
and shear 300 sheep.

were no islanders except the gulls and the penguins, the
sealions and the ducks, and the many other birds and
animals who still live there. It was a nature reserve; an
island innocent of man, knowing only the cries of birds
and the whispers and screams of the wind, and the cold,
ceaseless washing of the sea. When man finally came, he
was already civilized. And so, today, the people of the
islands have no ancient traditions; they have no legends,
gods or customs which recall the hardships and glories
of old. They are, conversely, a limb of modern civilization; widely separated and remote, yet close: wearing the
clothes of their cousins in England and Scotland and
Wales, speaking the same language.

But an Englishman can never be so close to a Kelper
that he understands the meaning of his isolation on the
Falkland Islands. This is, above all else, the feature of
island life which affects all its inhabitants. Whether a
life-long Kelper – who is often suspicious of outsiders –
or a visitor only in the Falklands for a short time, the
loneliness is inescapable. Old Kelpers, especially those
in the *camp*, achieve a self-sufficiency almost forgotten
by their cousins in England. They have the 'box', the radio,
for communication with others in the Falklands. Only
a few of the wives yearn for greater contact and easier
transport. Among those who make the Falklands their
home for a short time, perhaps there on Government
commissions, boredom is the most common trial. Social
life is sorely lacking even in Stanley.

The shepherd who lives in a tiny house, alone on one of
the tiny islands with only a thousand sheep for company,
must be a special kind of man. He has heard what
England is like – perhaps he has been there – but it is still
this lonely life that he prefers. Some of the older
Kelpers resist all efforts to bring greater contact with
others to them. And in Stanley, the only town of the
Falklands (though it is not more than a village by other
standards), a sense of remoteness from the world is
inevitable. The thin streets with low houses do not
seem to have captured a community; a dozen shops are
scattered, not collected in a center. An artificial creation
on the slope of a hill, surrounded by a barren moor-
scape, Stanley hardly lives up to its status as a cathedral
city, the British Commonwealth's most southerly town.
Roads leaving the town come to an abrupt end just
outside its boundaries.

The difference between the townspeople and the farmers is remarkable in such a small community. Stanley is
a source of interest which draws the remote islanders
together and is the main topic of conversation in the
camp – as the town dwellers call the rest of the main
island and smaller islands. Yet the citizens of Stanley
seem uninterested in what goes on outside. They work in
government departments, or for the Company, or for one
of the two research stations on the island. The town
people will not enquire how it is on the farm, yet from
there comes their peat, and the wool from the sheep

which is the source of their income.

It would be wrong to say that the islanders were
wealthy, though they are by the standards of many other
island communities. More to the point is that the good
income they receive from the woolen and trading
activities is difficult to spend. Rather than on smart
clothes, restaurants and parties, money is spent on domestic appliances like washing machines and refrigerators
powered by home generators. For the farmers in remote
parts there is always enough money to pay for a flight to
Stanley. The aircraft which are used for these flights are
two Beavers, fitted with floats for sea operation (there
are no landing strips on the islands). Flights are irregular
and news of arrivals and departures is broadcast on the
'box' – the islands' radio transmitter service – inter-
spersed with messages and ancient taped programs from
the BBC. Mail, supplies and passengers are all delivered
by Beavers.

In a community so well served with amenities and
affluence, there are certain anomalies which seem out

The settlement at Roy Cove is about 90 years old. The wool from its sheep realizes the best price at the London wool auctions.

(Bottom) Christchurch cathedral in Stanley allows this town of 1,000 people the title of 'the Commonwealth's most southerly cathedral city'.

of place, almost primitive. There is for instance the peat, which is dug during the spring and summer. It is a communal activity: for the farmers on the islands and in remote parts of East and West Falkland it is merely a matter of digging it anywhere, but each household in Stanley is allotted a peat bog of about 150 yards. The sods are cut with a spade, each one about the size of a brick. They are then 'ricked' or laid out so that the wind can get to them and make them dry and shrink. Finally the peat sods are carted home by lorry and carried in old paraffin drums to the peat shed – a feature of every house – where they are stored. The early settlers like the Chelsea Pensioners, did the same, though they used horse-drawn carts instead of lorries. Only a few of the islanders have installed central heating which uses other fuel. Oil is expensive to import and peat can be used in many boilers and stoves. But it is a dirty, dusty fuel which soils the bright clean colors of Falkland houses. However, as it is sometimes said, if it were not for the peat cutting, Kelpers would not know how to occupy their spare time.

For many of the people, however, sheep are a full-time occupation. The people of Weddell Island, like most of the other small islands, are entirely devoted to them. The only way to get there is by the Beaver (providing the aircraft are not wind-bound) which skims to a halt in a calm harbor just in front of the settlement. It is a small place; just a few houses, out-buildings and a cookhouse; with only the manager, his foreman, five shepherds, the cowman, cook and their families. Five minutes walk away is the 'big house' in which the manager lives with his wife and children. This was built in the latter part of the 19th century and is comfortable and warm. Electric power comes from a generator, but operates only between sunset and an hour before midnight. For all the men the day is taken up with the sheep – the gathering and shearing, which begin in November, the dipping which begins in February, the lamb marking, the wool pressing. The work entails traveling across the island by horseback, and sailing to the neighboring Beaver Island, where the single hermit shepherd protects his flock from the islands' only predators – long-haired foxes – who once reduced the flock from 10,000 to 7,000.

There is much wildlife on all the islands. Penguins are as much a part of island life as the sheep. Penguin eggs are eaten with relish by most farmers in the camp. They are hardboiled, shelled and served with melted butter. The translucent white has a delicious fish flavor. On Weddell there are four colonies of gentoo penguins and elsewhere the numbers are even greater. Living in apparently overcrowded conditions, each nest is only three feet from its neighbor. In the penguin colonies, the grass is gone, replaced by a stretch of brown, slimy earth which stinks from the birds' dung. And yet they are sedate creatures, strutting upright to shuffle and waddle to the water, where they become sleek and quick, black

and white arrows beneath the surface. Skuas and oyster-catchers, ducks and geese, seals and sealions proliferate around the coasts or inland; in the sea there are also the dolphins and porpoises, showing off with quick flashes of their fins.

Falkland islanders will show off their islands with pride. They will look out on slopes and lowlands covered in coarse grass and *diddle dee* (a kind of heather), on windswept heaths with outcrops of quartz rock, and on the peat bogs which can vary in color from green to dark purple, and barely give a thought to the extraordinary quiet that falls upon the islands when the wind drops. The silence is uncanny.

Falkland islanders are so often remote from one another, isolated on their farms in the *camp* or on one of the tiny islands, that theirs is, in many ways, an artificial community. With little history or tradition to share, and little contact with each other (except in Stanley, although many of the townspeople are only there on short commissions), there is an ingrained Kelper identity only among those who share a deep affection for the Falkland way of life. Those who enjoy isolation and a certain remoteness from the world are the true Kelpers.

The Hebrides and the lost St Kildans

On their lonely isles off
Scotland's west coast, Outer
Hebrideans are an ageing
community. Death claims the
old, the mainland the young.

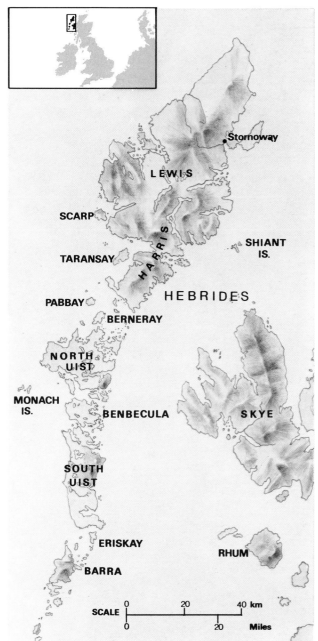

The clan communities of the Hebridean Islands off the north-west coast of Scotland have been declining for well over a century, although on the larger islands such as Lewis and Skye modernized industries and amenities have helped to preserve the spirit of the hardy island people.

But the great blow to the islanders was an economic one: the potato blight of the mid-19th century, and then the need of the lairds and clan chiefs to graze ever increasing flocks of blackfaced sheep on their traditional 127

ATLANTIC **Outer Hebrideans**

As big estates replaced the clan system, many crofters had to give way to the black faced sheep, and left by the hundred for Canada and the U.S.

Despite the isolation and low income, some crofters stay on their beloved isles, held by a blend of inertia and loyalty to their heritage.

The sea and its shores are a constant source of food — big worms at low tide for long-line bait; saithe and codling; and mackerel for lobster creels.

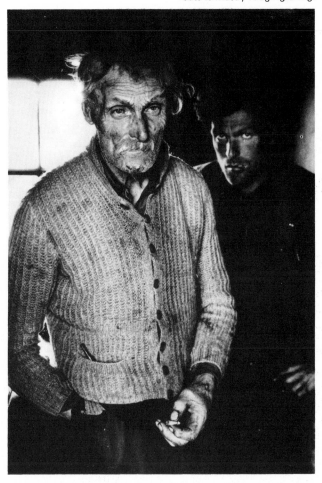

These fishermen of Işlay make a good living. Yet the land which used to be intensively cultivated with potatoes and oats is mostly rough grazing.

lands in order to keep going. Islanders in their thousands departed for the mainland or for newer worlds. For example, virtually the entire population of the Island of Rhum transhipped themselves to Cape Breton Island in the Gulf of St Lawrence in the 1890s. With the shock of dispersal, the old island crafts began to lapse. Wool spinning and weaving have survived successfully only in Harris. Modern chemistry overtook the trade in kelp (seaweed) ash for iodine manufacture. The ubiquitous 'lazy beds', where the peaty earth was scraped up in lumps for growing potatoes and oats, fell into disuse. The many-hooked long lines were no longer laid along the sea bed at nights. Government welfare more and more propped up the islanders and their economy. But a few new industries – lobster and scallop fishing, herring fishing, kipper curing and tourists – now seem to have a secure place among the larger communities.

Yet the harshest penalties of isolation from an ever more intrusive mainland culture have been, and are being, paid by the smaller and more remote island communities. Of these, the most far flung of all was always St Kilda – a community that died. At the time of writing only 14 of the once flourishing population of St Kilda are still alive – scattered throughout Britain, and one in Canada.

As long as St Kilda remained remote from the world, its society survived, but in the 19th century this tiny Hebridean island, stranded far out in the Atlantic, was discovered by missionaries, do-gooders and tourists. Under the impression that they were bringing the benefits of civilization they brought money, disease and despotism. The St Kildans could not withstand the effects of increased contact with the mainland and their culture slowly disintegrated. The population dwindled and in 1930 the islanders were no longer able to support themselves and had to be evacuated to the Scottish mainland.

The archipelago of St Kilda, which consists of Hirta, Soay, Boreray and Dun, lies on the edge of the continental shelf 50 miles due west of the large Hebridean island of Harris. Cliff-bound and surrounded by deep water, the islands are as inaccessible as they are isolated. The people depended for their survival on the enormous colonies of gannets, fulmar and puffins. The birds provide the land with fertilizer and the sea with plankton from their guano. On Hirta, the largest of the islands, there are numerous fresh-water springs. Lush-green and fertile, it was an ideal place to settle.

The early history of St Kilda follows roughly the same pattern as other Hebridean islands. Stone Age settlers, Celtic invaders, early Christians and Vikings succeeded each other without really altering the islanders' way of life. Druidism gave ritual to the St Kilda's close relationship with nature, while early Christianity did the same for his relationship with his fellow men.

For most of its history St Kilda was a self-supporting commonwealth. From the end of the 14th century until 1930 it belonged to the MacLeods of Dunvegan from Skye. The islanders had to produce enough surplus to pay the rent. A MacLeod steward visited the island once a year to see to the islanders' needs and collect the rent, which they paid chiefly in the oil, feathers and dried carcasses of sea-birds. Imports were kept down to bare necessities. Paying the rent was the responsibility of the whole community. Arable land, fowling cliffs, boats and ropes were all held in common. Land was divided into plots and portions and rotated among the island's families at regular intervals.

Decisions on the welfare of the community were taken by the Parliament made up of all the grown males on the island. They met every morning to decide what work should be done that day. There was next to no crime on the island and disputes were easily settled. The island laws were mostly concerned with the division of property and the administration of justice in sharing it out. The Parliament ensured that no islander was raised above another. Satisfied with their own arrangement the St Kildans never registered a vote which helped send a man to Westminster as member of the British Parliament.

There were about 200 St Kildans at the end of the 17th 12

These St Kildans of 1890
were already becoming less
self-reliant. In 1931 their
tiny community, of 36, broken
in spirit, was shipped out.

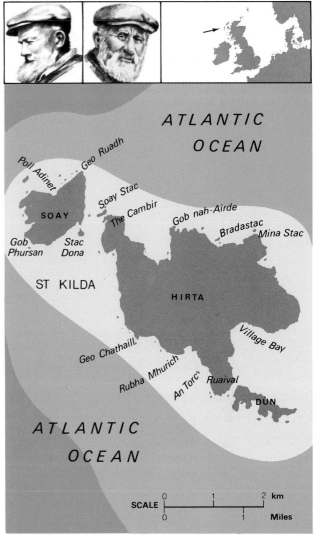

century. They lived in a long row of black houses, called 'the street.' Some of the earlier houses were of a beehive type, like the many stone cleits dotted about the island in which the people stored and dried their food. Although their cows lived with them in their houses in winter and manure was prepared on the floor, the houses were warm and dry and comfortable.

The islanders lived off a diet of fulmar, gannets and puffins which they ate either fresh in season or cured out of season. In 1696 they consumed 22,600 gannets though this was considered a poor year. At one time the fulmar's oil was in great demand as a medicine on the mainland and its feathers were sold as stuffing for mattresses.

Both gannets and fulmar were hunted when young, before they could fly. Puffins were taken fully grown and had to be caught with fowling rods or snares or sometimes dogs which pulled them out of their burrows.

13

The St Kildan isle of Hirta
and its satellites lie over
40 miles west of Harris
and Uist in the Atlantic.
Once, 180 lived there serenely.

ATLANTIC **Outer Hebrideans**

St Kildan ladies of 1890,
each with characteristic
white frills to their caps,
gossip in The Street, the
island's single row of houses.

Overseas mail from St Kilda
went by bottles thrown into
the ocean and washed up,
with luck, on the shores of
Lewis, Harris or the Uists.

Ruined crofts and the tall
crags where men bravely
clambered after birds are
the sole testimony to St
Kilda's dead community.

Fowling was St Kilda's most important activity. A man who was no good at climbing was no good to the island and was unlikely to survive, and so boys received their education on the cliffs from an early age. By the time they were 16 they were fully-fledged cragsmen.

A young St Kildan could not marry before he had shown that he was capable of supporting a wife by displaying his courage and skill as a cragsman – in the ritual of the Mistress Stone. The potential bridegroom had to balance on the heel of one foot on the edge of a flat rock overlooking a sheer 250 foot drop to the sea below, and hold this position until his friends decided that he had proved himself.

In the days when risks were taken for risk's sake climbing accidents were common, and often fatal. Later, fatal accidents became rare. The islanders would tell dramatic stories of the dangers of fowling which encouraged the islanders to believe in themselves and their ability to survive, and perpetuated the myth of the heroic cragsman.

The islanders used the few boats that they owned mostly for fowling and for tending sheep on the other islands in the group. They were cautious sailors and kept to their own waters, which, although well stocked, they seldom fished.

Although farming provided a substantial part of the islanders' diet and contributed produce towards the rent, it was another secondary occupation. They cultivated barley, corn and oats on 50 to 100 acres; but the summers were short, the harvest always had to be gathered quickly in case of storms and the St Kildans were anyway more interested in livestock than in crops. They owned a small herd of cattle and about 1,500 sheep on Hirta and Boreray. The sheep on Soay and the Dun, which belonged to MacLeod, were a pure primitive breed probably descended from the wild moufflon and were only caught for their wool. The islanders' own mixed-bred sheep which were wild and agile, never flocked together and had to be caught individually by specially trained dogs. They were killed for meat in autumn and on feast days.

In winter the St Kildans busied themselves making tweed to clothe themselves and for export. The men were traditionally the island's tailors, but the women had to work hard at other jobs, especially those which involved carrying. One of the island's unmarried women was their queen and led the female puffin snaring expeditions to Boreray in summer. It is possible that St Kilda was once a matriarchal society: there is too a story about a female warrior; and there are certain oddities in the division of labor between the sexes.

Life in St Kilda was certainly simple and severe but the islanders were nevertheless well fed, well clothed and well housed.

In the 18th century St Kilda was romanticized as a kind of utopia though very few outsiders had actually been

St Kildans lived on fulmar, gannets and puffins. Here they divide the catch of fulmar, whose oil was used by Scots as a medicine.

Till 1889 the Rev John Mackay, 'a holy bigot,' set up harsh rule over St Kildans and undermined their strength of spirit.

there. As late as 1850 the St Kildans had never seen rabbits, rats, pigs, bees or fruit. Their ignorance and naivety became legendary, and confused with estimates of their moral worth.

The St Kildans received foreigners with a mixture of fear and delight. They were always hospitable although they knew that contact with strangers tended to cause the whole community to catch 'the stranger's cough', a severe form of influenza to which the islanders had little immunity. In 1724 the community was almost wiped out by an epidemic of smallpox.

As contact with the mainland increased and the world began its bid to bring St Kilda into line with the rest of civilization, things began to go wrong. The St Kildans' survival depended on their isolation.

First came the missionaries. Because of the people's natural religiosity and superstitious nature, the missionaries were able to set themselves up as the islanders' spiritual dictators without opposition. By their superior knowledge they gained an easy ascendancy over the hearts and minds of the islanders. Their authority spread into every St Kildan activity.

Although a few missionaries came to St Kilda in the 18th century it was not until the Rev John MacDonald, the 'Apostle of the North', arrived in 1822 that the islanders were first subjected to dogmatic Christianity. He was succeeded by the Reverend Neil Mackenzie, who worked hard to raise the islanders' standard of living. He reorganized their farming, persuaded them to rebuild their village and reinstated education. Although he did not neglect the islanders' spiritual health he was an enlightened leader. He confronted them with change and progress and advanced their material prosperity. But when he went away in 1844 he left behind a newly created dependency and a vacuum.

It was filled by the Reverend John Mackay, a holy bigot, who quickly established a vibrantly harsh 24 years' long rule over his parishioners. His sabbatarianism was so extreme that the St Kildans, forced to attend three services on Sunday and prayer meetings most days of the week, were prevented from doing their work. He banned singing and dancing, poetry, story-telling and sport. The island was drowned, apparently for ever, in a sea of oppressive salvationism. The St Kildans did not even try to resist this puritanical orthodoxy; they accepted it as inevitable and right.

With further contact with civilization, the islanders became susceptible to diseases previously unknown in St Kilda. By the 20th century a general debilitating weakness had set in. More than any other disease, *tetanus infantum* contributed to the decline of the community: it killed new-born children usually within a week of birth. In the middle of the 19th century, eight out of ten children died of tetanus. By 1890 it had been brought under control but the cost of the population over the century was never recovered. The emigration

to Australia in the 1850s of 42 islanders may have sealed the fate of the community.

Unable to adapt to the changing needs of the modern world, the economy of St Kilda collapsed towards the end of the 19th century. The mainland demand for sea-bird products had fallen away and the islanders had run down their agriculture until they could not even produce enough food for their own needs. They were able to make a little – but not enough – money from tourists and by selling tweed. As their exports diminished their imports increased. The St Kildans were no longer self-supporting and came to rely more and more on charity.

Tourism had an equally malign effect. From total isolation the St Kildans were suddenly over-exposed. The visitors' curiosity tended to be scornful and the islanders began to lose respect for their own customs and rituals. The 'steamer season' became the most important in the islanders' year. Once money could be earned from tourists, getting more of it became a necessity. The islanders' needs and tastes became more sophisticated. They bought food and other things from outside, and became even more dependent on communications with the mainland. Unfortunately tourism was an unstable source of revenue. By the beginning of the 20th century the Victorian vogue for St Kilda had died.

Communications with the mainland improved enough to destroy St Kilda's independence, but not enough to bring St Kilda into the swim of Scottish life. Isolated but no longer self-reliant, survival became almost impossible. As early as 1875 evacuation had been suggested as a solution, but the community had preferred to struggle on. In 1913 the islanders, on the point of starvation and laid low by an influenza epidemic, were saved by World War I. A Navy signal station was established on the island and for four years the St Kildans enjoyed a false prosperity.

When the war ended and the Navy signal station was disbanded, many of the old people died and most of the young men left the island. The population fell from 73 in 1920 to 37 in 1928. Life was reduced to a miserable level. In 1929 an epidemic of wet eczema coincided with the harvest, which remained ungathered: the St Kildans were once again threatened with famine. On 10 May 1930 they signed a petition to the Secretary of State for Scotland asking to be removed from the island. They were settled on the mainland.

The St Kildans were given homes and jobs in Morvern, Argyll. The community gradually dispersed. The younger people suffered less from the pains of adjustment. Those still alive today regard the evacuation of St Kilda as inevitable. They could not have survived another winter. The community had been living on borrowed time since the turn of the century and it had long been clear that the advantages of the outside world would never come to St Kilda, where life could neither go forwards nor backwards, for it had long since come to a stop.

Though British, St Kildans
never sent a man to the
London parliament, for the
island had its own. Here it
gathers before a debate.

13

(Left and right) At a
Glasgow hotel, the seven
survivors of the dead St
Kilda community reunite
with nostalgia, after 41 years.

Glossary to the Caribbean and Atlantic islanders

In the Caribbean and the Atlantic islands, most populations are of recent standing. In the Caribbean most are of African ancestry, for during the slave trade era some nine million African slaves reached the West Indies and America. Today there are very few of the million Amerindians (mainly Arawaks and Caribs) that Columbus found in the 1490's. The other people in the Caribbean are Europeans, Americans and Asians. Some are descended from those who came as planters or indentured workers four centuries ago, a few are the descendants of British loyalist refugees from the American War of Independence and some have settled more recently as business men or pleasure seekers. Of the Atlantic islands some, like the Shetlands and the Faroes, have a long history of a continuous population. Some like the Azores, remained uninhabited until the Portuguese discovered them and settled there. Others, like the Canaries, had an indigenous population that was assimilated by the colonizing Spaniards. A few are peopled only at certain times of year like the Falkland Island Dependencies, while others remain uninhabited because they are too small, too remote, or too cold.

ANDROS (see BAHAMAS) *Population:* 7,500. Language: English. The island is the largest in the Bahamas – 1,600 square miles. It lies 140 miles south-east of Florida. The soil is infertile, and the population – largely negro – rely for most of their income on cutting timber (pine and mahogany) and on fishing. Andros town was built specifically as a tourist resort.

ANGUILLA *Population:* 6,000. Language: English. Direct British rule. This Snake Island, so called because of its shape, is one of the Leeward Islands in the Lesser Antilles. It is 60 miles north-west of St Kitts, whose domination it vehemently resisted in the late 1960s. It is only 35 square miles, and was colonized by the British in the 17th century. The island is generally too dry for agriculture. Charcoal burners have destroyed all the trees. The mainly negro population exports salt and lime, but much of the islanders' income is from young Anguillans who work abroad.

ANTIGUA *Population:* 63,000. Language: English. British Associated State. At the southern end of the Leeward Islands chain, Antigua covers 171 square miles. Antigua is one of the earliest British settlements in the West Indies, colonized in 1632. The people of this low-lying, semi-arid, limestone island now work on plantations and produce sugar-cane, cotton and molasses. There are also rum distilleries and oil refineries.

ANTILLES 'The Antilles' is now a geographical term which covers the whole of the West Indies except the Bahamas. The name comes from the legendary island of Antilia, connected perhaps with Plato's Atlantis. The 'Greater Antilles' is the geographical name for the chain of large islands (such as Cuba, Jamaica, Hispaniola and Puerto Rico) that lie to the north-west of the Lesser Antilles, the crescent of many smaller islands which geographers divide into two groups, the Windward and Leeward Islands.

ASCENSION *Population:* 500. Language: English. A British colony with St Helena. Ascension, 34 square miles, is in the Atlantic 700 miles north-west of St Helena. Discovered by the Portuguese in 1501, it remained uninhabited until occupied by the

British in 1815 as a safeguard against Napoleon's escape from St Helena. Although the island is largely barren, the people raise some pigs, sheep and cattle, and grow fruit and vegetables on a few acres. The island is a missile-tracking and cable station.

THE AZORES *Population:* 340,000. Language: Portuguese. District of Portugal. The volcanic islands of the Azores, 924 square miles, are 740 miles west of Portugal in the north Atlantic. They divide into three separate groups: the north-eastern group of São Miguel, Santa Maria and Formigas; the central group of Faial, Pico, São Jorge Tercera and Graciosa; and in the north-west, Flores and Carvo. At first only a group of rocks were known, and christened 'Ants' (Formigas), but in 1432 Gincale Velso Cabral found the island of Santa Maria only 15 miles from the Formigas. By the end of the century all the islands were peopled. The present inhabitants, mostly Portuguese in origin, cultivate pineapples under glass, and fish for tuna, mullet and bonito. The Azores are a cable, airway and weather center.

BAHAMAS *Population:* 170,000. Language: English. Independent within the British Commonwealth. The Bahamas form a chain of islands and reefs of 4,404 square miles that stretch for 760 miles south-east from Grand Bahama to Inagua (near the eastern end of Cuba). They include Great and Little Abaco,

Andros, Inagua, Grand Bahama, New Providence, Eleuthera, Exuma, San Salvador and Acklins, Long and Crooked Islands (*q.v.*). The Bahamas were discovered by Columbus in 1492, the first American discovery. They were a haven for smugglers and for English loyalists during the American War of Independence. 25% of the population are of European origin, or of mixed blood: the remaining 75% are negro descendants of African slaves. The dominating industry is tourism. Olives, fruit, indigo, coffee, sisal and spices are main products. The people exploit the hardwood forests, catch game-birds, fish for turtles and dive for sponges. They export cement, rum, pulpwood, crawfish and salt.

BARBADOS *Population:* 253,000. Language: English. Independent within the British Commonwealth. 100 miles east of St Vincent, Barbados is the most easterly of the West Indies. It was settled by the British during the early 17th century although most of the present population are of African and mixed descent and only 5% are of European origin. Since the mid-17th century the people on this island of only 166 square miles have largely depended on exporting sugar and rum. They now also produce plastics and electrical goods, and their tourist trade has expanded. **(pages 50-55)**

BARBUDA *Population:* 1,200. Language: English. Dependency of Antigua – British Associated State. This low-lying coral island is 25 miles north of Antigua, has an area of only 62 square miles and was colonized in 1628. The farming land is poor and largely covered with dense scrub; most of the people live by fishing, keeping cattle and making charcoal.

BAY ISLANDS *Population:* 11,000. Language: mainly English. Part of the republic of Honduras since 1859. Most of the inhabitants of this small archipelago in the bay of Honduras are white, and are descended from 17th and 18th century British pirates and mutineers. Communications with Trujillo on the mainland of Honduras are erratic, but the neighboring islands of Bonacca and Utila are easily accessible by boat. The main products are coconuts and bananas, while the chief industry is boat building. Roatan, on an island of the same name, is the chief port. **(pages 64-69)**

BERMUDA (THE BERMUDA ISLANDS) *Population:* 55,000. Language: English. Self-governing British colony. This group of about 300 islands covers only 200 square miles in the north Atlantic, 570 miles east of the U.S. Bermuda has one of the highest population densities in the world. It was colonized by the English who imported slaves and, later, Portuguese laborers. 65% of the people are negroes and mulattos. For many years the inhabitants lived by ship-building and growing food crops but now the islands have become a tax-haven and tourist center. They export lily-buds, oils and perfumes, and have started a pharmaceutical industry.

CANARY ISLANDS *Population:* 950,000. Languages: Spanish, Spanish dialect. This Spanish archipelago is 2,800 square miles, and about 70 miles from the north-west African mainland. The western group includes the mountainous Tenerife, Grand Canary, Palma, Gomera and Hierro, while in the lower-lying eastern group there are Fuertaventura, Lanzarote and six islets. The islanders, mainly of Spanish and some of Guanche origin, vary from tall and blue-eyed in the west to small and dark in the east. They cultivate tomatoes, bananas and other fruits; they fish for tuna and sardines; and they cater for tourism. **(pages 100-111)**

CAPE VERDE ISLANDS *Population:* 293,000. Languages: Portuguese, Guinea tribal languages. Portuguese Province. This crescent-shaped archipelago, of 1,557 square miles, is 280 miles off the African coast. The Portuguese settled there in 1460 and brought in negroes from Guinea to work on their plantations. A strong African influence is visible in the people, 72% of whom are negroes and mulattos, and many of whom still practise animist religions. The people produce coffee, nuts, cereals. They keep animals, especially goats, and they fish for tuna and extract salt from the sea.

CAYMAN ISLANDS *Population:* 7,800. Language: English. British Associated State. These coral islands are 200 miles north-west of Jamaica and include Grand Cayman, Little Cayman and Cayman Brac. About one third of the people are white, half are mulatto and only one sixth are negro. Nearly all are in some way descended from English colonists, and from Africans who came from Jamaica in the 18th century. The islanders are by tradition fishermen, turtlers, and merchant seamen in foreign ships. They have an increasing income from tourism.

CUBA *Population:* 8 million. Language: Spanish. Independent republic. The largest of the Greater Antilles, Cuba has an area of 44,220 square miles, including many small islands. Since 1959 the people's social, economic and political life has been dominated by what they call Revolutionary Communism. The island's foreign relations, which until recently centered on the US, are now principally with the USSR. 73% of the people are of European (largely Spanish) origin, 26% negro and mulatto and 1% Chinese. Most of the people work on the land, which is richly fertile and yields more sugar than any country in the world after the USSR. They also grow tobacco, coffee, rice and other food crops, and mine metal ores. **(pages 16-27)**

CURAÇAO (see NETHERLANDS ANTILLES) *Population:* 130,000. Language: Dutch. Curaçao (173 square miles) is the largest island of the Netherlands Antilles. The island is dry and largely barren. The inhabitants, mainly negroes, grow the special Curaçao orange used in making Curaçao liqueur, and weave straw hats. The dis- 1

Between 1450 and 1850 about 9¼ million African slaves were transported across the Atlantic by the Middle Passage. The map shows what percentage of their number went to each of the various Caribbean destinations. Not until the vast European migrations to North America of the 19th and 20th centuries did so many people move across the world.

Slavery was well established in Africa before the Portuguese discovered the route to West Africa at the end of the 15th century. The slave traders, principally Arabs, regarded slaves not only as a convenient way of managing the complex Muslim household, but also as potential converts to Islam. Christian traders later used the same argument: slavery would benefit both their own pockets and the soul of the slave.

The Portuguese and shortly afterwards the Dutch, Danes, English and other Europeans established themselves further and further south on the West African coast: and as they moved westwards, first to the Azores and eventually to the New World, they took with them, ready-made, the idea of slave-operated sugar plantations.

The New World Indians proved unsuitable for work on the plantations: many died of European diseases to which they had no natural resistance. Meanwhile the West African traders were sailing down the coast of Africa on the 'trade winds' as they came to be called; as it was difficult to battle back northwards against these winds, the trading ships would then strike out westwards – to the Azores, or, finally, to the Caribbean – and complete the triangular voyage by returning on prevailing winds that blew east across the Atlantic towards Europe.

To make this long voyage doubly profitable, the traders hit upon the idea of taking as payment for the goods they brought to Africa – the cloth, alcohol, beads and knives – a shipload of slaves, to be sold to the West Indies, Brazil or North America. This human cargo was swopped for sugar and rum from the Caribbean, or later for North American tobacco or cotton. A successful trip could yield enormous profits.

This trade prospered in the 18th century when sugar became less profitable, and some plantations went bankrupt. It was perhaps not entirely coincidental that at this time too began the movement to abolish slavery.

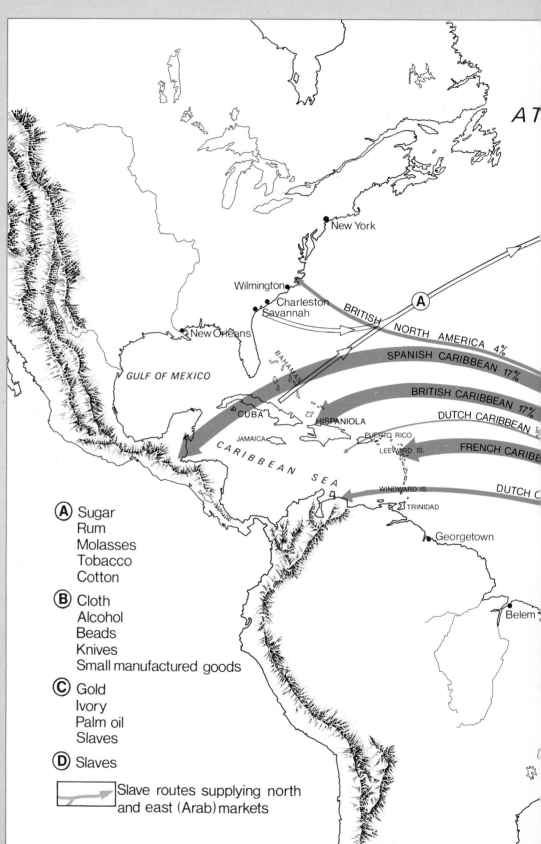

AT

New York

Wilmington
Charleston
Savannah

New Orleans

GULF OF MEXICO

BAHAMAS

CUBA

HISPANIOLA

JAMAICA

PUERTO RICO

LEEWARD IS.

WINDWARD IS.

TRINIDAD

Georgetown

CARIBBEAN SEA

BRITISH NORTH AMERICA 4%

SPANISH CARIBBEAN 17%

BRITISH CARIBBEAN 17%

DUTCH CARIBBEAN ½

FRENCH CARIBE

DUTCH C

Belem

Ⓐ Sugar
Rum
Molasses
Tobacco
Cotton

Ⓑ Cloth
Alcohol
Beads
Knives
Small manufactured goods

Ⓒ Gold
Ivory
Palm oil
Slaves

Ⓓ Slaves

Slave routes supplying north and east (Arab) markets

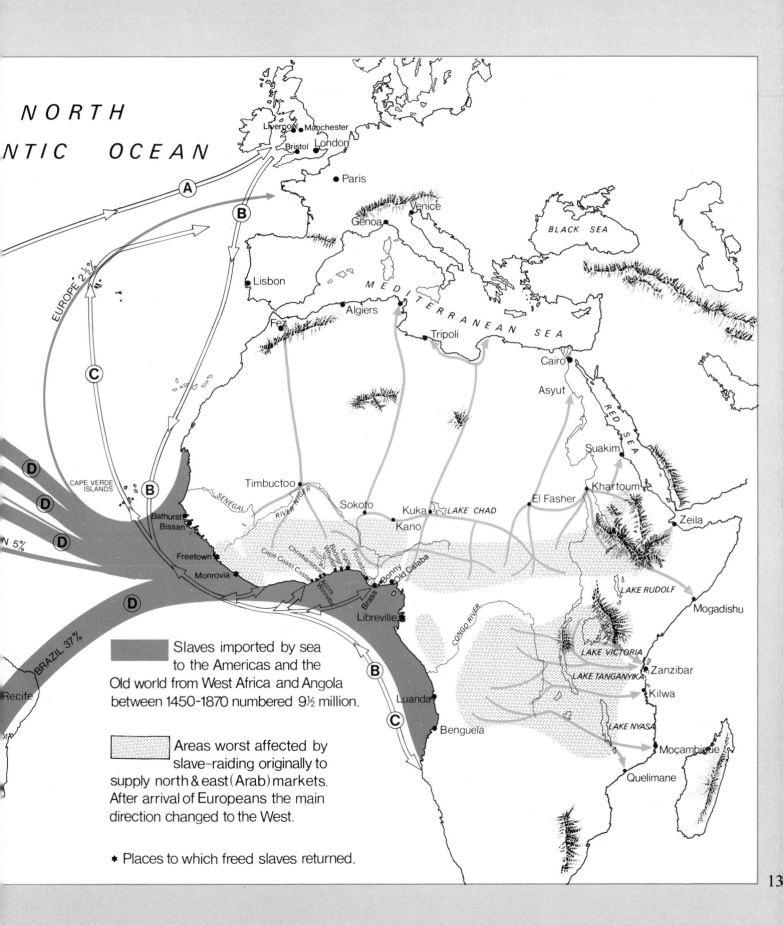

NORTH

NTIC OCEAN

Ⓐ

Ⓑ

Liverpool Manchester

Bristol London

Paris

Venice

Genoa

BLACK SEA

EUROPE 2½%

Ⓒ

Lisbon

M E D I T E R R A N E A N   S E A

Algiers

Fez

Tripoli

Cairo

Asyut

RED SEA

Ⓓ

Suakim

CAPE VERDE
ISLANDS

Ⓑ

Khartoum

Timbuctoo

Ⓓ

RIVER NIGER

Sokoto

El Fasher

Zeila

SENEGAL

Kuka *LAKE CHAD*

Ⓓ

N 5%

Bathurst
Bissan

Kano

Freetown

Christiansborg
Bonny

Monrovia

Cape Coast Castle

Focodou

Old Calaba

Ⓓ

Accra Winneba

Brass

LAKE RUDOLF

Libreville

Mogadishu

CONGO RIVER

Slaves imported by sea
to the Americas and the
Old world from West Africa and Angola
between 1450-1870 numbered 9½ million.

LAKE VICTORIA

Ⓑ

Zanzibar

LAKE TANGANYIKA

BRAZIL 37%

Luanda

Kilwa

Recife

Ⓒ

Benguela

LAKE NYASA

Areas worst affected by
slave-raiding originally to
supply north & east (Arab) markets.
After arrival of Europeans the main
direction changed to the West.

Moçambique

Quelimane

★ Places to which freed slaves returned.

13

covery of oil in 1916 in Venezuela, 40 miles to the south, brought oil refineries, prosperity, and immigrants from other islands – and political strains.

DOMINICA *Population:* 77,000. Languages: English, French *patois.* A self-governing British Associated State. 290 square miles in area, Dominica is one of the Lesser Antilles' Windward Isles, and lies midway between Guadeloupe and Martinique. Its fierce native Caribs, who fought from the forested mountains, delayed conquest until well into the 18th century – about 400 pure Caribs survive in the island today. Since the land is unsuitable for growing sugar-cane, few negro slaves were imported and so the population, although mainly negro, has never been large. Heavy rainfall allows the people, mostly smallholders, to grow bananas and citrus fruits. Tourism is making the islanders more prosperous.
(pages 42-49)

DOMINICAN REPUBLIC *Population:* 4.5 million. Language: Spanish. The Dominican Republic, the site of the first Spanish settlement in the Americas, shares the island of Hispaniola with Haiti, from which it separated in 1844. Of the present population, 28% are of mainly Spanish descent, 60% are mulatto or *mestizo* and 11% are negro. The people cultivate most of the country's 18,720 square miles with crops of sugar, cocoa, coffee, rice, tobacco and bananas. They also produce beer, bauxite, iron ore, cement, glass and textiles.

ELEUTHERA (see BAHAMAS) *Population:* 8,000. Language: English. This long, narrow Bahamian island (164 square miles) lies about 200 miles east of Florida. The island was settled in 1647 by the Company of Eleutheran Adventurers from London, and became the resort of loyalists who fled America during the War of Independence. Though the island has some large modern livestock farms, fishing is the main occupation of the largely negro population.

FALKLAND ISLANDS *Population:* 2,100. Language: English. British colony. East and West Falkland, with 200 smaller islands, are 250 miles east of South America in the south

Atlantic, and have an area of 6,200 square miles. They were discovered by an English navigator in 1592, but were not settled until 1764. Only about a dozen of the islands are inhabited. The people produce wool for export, and depend on external supply for everything but meat, fish and vegetables.
(pages 120-125)

FALKLAND ISLANDS DEPENDENCIES *Population:* fluctuates between 100 and 1,300. Language: English. These 12 south Atlantic islands, which include South Georgia and the South Sandwich Islands, have been Dependencies of the Falkland Islands since 1908. South Georgia, the main island, is glacier-topped. It is 700 miles east of the Falklands, and was first sighted in 1775. It was used as a whaling station in the 19th century but now has no permanent population. The people who live there are employed mainly in summer, either on the space-tracking station or on scientific bases. The South Sandwich Islands are an uninhabited group of volcanic islands strung out over 200 miles.

THE FAROES *Population:* 38,000. Language: Faroese (a dialect of Old Norse). Self-governing state of Denmark. This group of 21 islands, 540 square miles, is about 200 miles north-west of Shetland. 17 of the rugged rainswept islands, of which Strömö is the most important, are inhabited by descendants of 9th century Norse settlers. There is some cultivation, animal rearing and knitting, but fishing has become the main trade.
(pages 82-91)

FERNANDO NORONHA *Population:* about 2,000. Language: Portuguese. Fernando Noronha, a wooded island of about 10 square miles, lies 225 miles north-east of Brazil, and is named after its discoverer and first owner, a Portuguese count who found the island in 1504. Until Brazil acquired it as a penal colony, the island was uninhabited. The present inhabitants, who produce fruit and guano (bird manure used as a fertilizer) are outnumbered by the military garrison and prisoners.

FERNANDO PÓO ISLAND *Population:* 72,000. Languages: Spanish, tribal lan-

guages. Area: 786 square miles. Part of the independent state of Equatorial Guinea, the island lies 25 miles off the Nigerian Coast. A Spanish province (together with Rio Muni) till 1968, the island was discovered by the Portuguese explorer Fernão do Po in 1472. The volcanic peak of Santa Isabel rises to 9,348 feet. The island's capital of Santa Isabel is capital of Equatorial Guinea. The indigenous people are of the Bubi tribe. They grow and export cocoa.

GRAND BAHAMA (see BAHAMAS) *Population:* 6,000, Language: English. Grand Bahama, some 430 square miles, lies about 70 miles east of Florida at the northern end of the Bahamas. Some English settled there in 1629. The people are mainly negroes, and live by fishing; they also export timber and pulpwood.

GRENADA *Population:* 105,000. Language: English. Self-governing British Associated State since 1967. Grenada, the southernmost of the Windward Islands, and formerly their capital, is 90 miles north of Trinidad in the eastern Caribbean. The predominantly negro population now cultivates two-thirds of the island's 133 square miles (on which the annual rainfall can be as much as 200 inches). The people produce bananas, cocoa, nutmeg, sugar and food crops for home consumption. They also mine sulphur and fuller's earth.

GRENADINES *Population:* 3,500. Language: English. The Grenadines, a group of over a hundred small islands, are among the Windward Islands, between Grenada in the north and St Vincent in the south. The islands south of Carriacou belong to Grenada, the rest to St Vincent. The islanders are mainly negro and live by subsistence farming and game-hunting. The larger islands of Carriacou (13 square miles) and Bequia (7 square miles) export cotton, limes, coconuts and grenadine – a distilled syrup of pomegranates or redcurrants.

GUADELOUPE *Population:* 350,000. Language: French. French colony. Guadeloupe is one of the Leeward Islands, and is 687 square miles in area. It consists principally of the twin islands of Basse-Terre and Grande-Terre on either side of a narrow

swampy sea-channel. Les Iles des Saintes, Marie-Galante, Petite-Terre and Désirade are dependencies which lie close by the main islands of Guadeloupe. When Columbus discovered Guadeloupe in 1493 it was occupied by Caribs, who were themselves relative newcomers. The islanders, descendants of French settlers and negro slaves, are intensely French in their loyalties. They grow bananas and sugar almost exclusively – and trade principally with France.
(pages 70-79)

HAITI *Population:* 5 million. Languages: French, French creole dialect. Haiti is the western third – about 10,700 square miles – of the island of Hispaniola (or Sainte Dominque) which it shares with the Dominican Republic. In the 18th century Haiti had the richest sugar plantations in the world, employing half a million slaves. The slave revolt in 1791 gained Haiti independence from France, and 90% of the present population are pure negro. The plantations disappeared with their owners, and today only a few coffee and sisal plantations remain. Most people profess Roman Catholicism – but also practise voodoo.
(pages 56-63)

HEBRIDES *Population:* 30,000. Languages: Gaelic, English. Part of Scotland. The Hebrides are a group of about 500 islands of which only 100 are inhabited. They are divided into the Outer and Inner Hebrides and have little sense of corporate identity: the people's loyalties go to their own islands. The chief islands of the Inner Hebrides are Skye, Mull, Jura, Islay, Coll, Colonsay, Tiree, Iona, Raasay, Scalpay, Canna, Rhum, Eigg and Muck. The chief islands of the Outer Hebrides are Lewis (with its southern portion of Harris), North and South Uist, and Barra. The once inhabited island of St Kilda lies furthest out into the Atlantic.
(pages 126-135)

ILES DES SAINTS (see GUADELOUPE) *Population:* small. Language: creole. The inhabitants of these six small islands to the south of Guadeloupe are the Bretons, who may have come originally from Brittany. Negro features are visible among them, but most are of brown-haired, fair-complexioned European stock. They are fishermen and skilled boat-builders. **(page 64-69)**

JAMAICA *Population:* 2,022,000. Languages: English, Spanish creole dialect. Indepent within the British Commonwealth. Jamaica (a British colony from 1655 until 1962) covers 4,413 square miles, and lies 90 miles south of eastern Cuba. 77% of the people are of African origin, 20% are mulatto and 3% are of European or Levantine origin. There are some Indians and Chinese. Jamaicans grow most kinds of tropical crop, especially sugar and bananas. The island has the largest bauxite deposits in the world. Despite increasing industrialization, the island's role as a playground of the rich contrasts sharply with overpopulation, poverty and illiteracy. **(pages 34-41)**

LEEWARD ISLANDS *Population:* 167,000. Languages: English, French, Dutch. All the islands that lie between Puerto Rico in the north and the Windward Islands in the south are collectively the Leeward Islands. They were to leeward of trading ships leaving the West Indies for Europe. Leeward Islands which have associations with Britain are Anguilla, the British Virgins (including Tortola, Virgin Gorda and Anegada), St Kitts, Nevis, Antigua, Montserrat, Dominica and Barbuda; French Leeward Islands are Martinique and its dependencies, Guadeloupe, St Bartholemew and part of St Martin; those associated with Holland are Saba, St Eustatius and the rest of St Martin; Leeward Islands with US associations are the US Virgins – St Croix, St Thomas and St John.

LEWIS AND HARRIS (see HEBRIDES) *Population:* 21,614 and 2,893. Languages: Gaelic, English. Part of Scotland. Lewis and Harris are in fact one island (of 859 square miles), the largest in the outer Hebrides, though Lewis is separated from Harris by a deep-sea loch and a fresh-water loch. Lewis is in the county of Ross and Cromarty, and Harris is in Inverness-shire, and Gaelic speakers notice a different 'tang' to the dialect spoken in the two parts of the island. The people live by crofting and by providing for the tourists drawn by the wild scenery and the game hunting on the island. 'Harris' tweed cloth, traditionally made by hand and named after the island, is manufactured by modern methods now mainly in Lewis.
(pages 130-135)

MADEIRA ISLANDS *Population:* 300,000. Language: Portuguese. Administrative district of Portugal. The Madeiras, 307 square miles in area, lie 570 miles south-west of Lisbon in the north Atlantic. Discovered in the 14th century by the Portuguese, they were colonized only after 1419. Today only the islands of Madeira and Porto Santo are inhabited. The people are of mixed Portuguese, Moorish and negro descent. Madeira wine has been exported to England since the 17th century, and the lace industry was started among the women and girls on the island by an English lady, Mrs Phelps, in the middle of the 19th century. The English were also the first to visit the island as tourists, attracted by its dry summers and profusion of flowers and birds. Apart from Madeira wine and lace, the people produce sugar and bananas, make wickerwork and fish for tuna.

MARGARITA *Population:* 75,000. Language: Spanish. Largest island of Nueva Esparta state of Venezuela. Isla de Margarita, 414 square miles in area, lies in the southern Caribbean 12 miles north of the Venezuelan mainland. Its famous pearl industry developed soon after its discovery by Columbus in 1498. The population are peasant farmers and are predominantly Indian with others of Spanish ancestry who originated chiefly from the Canary Islands. The women produce coarse straw hats. There are easily accessible deposits of high-quality magnesium.

MONTSERRAT *Population:* 15,000. Language: English. British crown colony. This jagged island, only 32 square miles, is one of the Leeward Islands and lies 27 miles southwest of Antigua. It was discovered by Columbus in 1493 and named after a Spanish mountain. Originally settled by Irish people in the 1630's, Montserrat's inhabitants are now predominantly negro. The land was impoverished by the early sugar plantations and now depends on cotton, the cash crop most susceptible to variations in the Caribbean climate and the least reliable. Only 7,000 acres are cultivable: the rest is bush which can support only shifting farming. The people have a long history of emigration, but this has declined since 1966.

MARTINIQUE *Population:* 365,000. Languages: French, creole dialect of French, English and Spanish. French colony since **14**

1674. Martinique, a volcanic island covering 420 square miles, is one of the Leeward Islands, and lies in the eastern Caribbean between Dominica and St Lucia. The present predominantly negro population vary from almost pure negro 'saccatra' to 'sangmélé' (of mixed descent). They live by growing cash crops of sugar, bananas, pineapples and coffee, and manufacture and export rum and Coca-Cola.
(pages 70-71)

NETHERLANDS ANTILLES *Population:* 200,000. Languages: Dutch, Papiamento (a composite of Dutch and Spanish), some English. Netherlands colony. Over 370 square miles in area, the Netherlands Antilles comprise two groups of the Lesser Antilles. The southern group – Curaçao, Aruba (*q.v.*) and Bonaire – lies 60 miles off the Venezuelan coast, in the Windward Islands. The northern group – Saba, Statia and the southern part of St Martin – is in the Leeward Islands. The population is mainly negro, with minorities of Portuguese, Dutch and Indians, but on Aruba two-thirds of the people are of Carib descent. Though the people grow some cotton and food crops, farming was always difficult on the islands, and most food has to be imported. Oil refining is now an important source of wealth.

NEVIS (see ST KITTS) *Population:* 15,000. Language: English. Part of British Associated State of St Kitts-Nevis. This small island 36 square miles in area, is in the Lesser Antilles two miles from St Kitts. Colonized by the English in 1628, the island experienced a sugar boom in the 18th century. The negro peasants grow enough food for their own and the island's needs, as well as coconuts and cotton for export.

NEWFOUNDLAND *Population:* 450,000. Languages: English, French. Part of Canada since 1949. This huge, triangular island, 42,734 square miles in area, stands off the great gulf of the St Lawrence river. For centuries the economy was based on cod-fishing. Colonization, principally by Irish and English people, was difficult: the land was so infertile, the weather so severe and the colonial regulations so draconian. Now mining for iron ore, lead, copper and zinc have brought increased prosperity, and the pulp and timber industries, using local hydro-electric power, exploit the forests that cover over half the island.
(pages 72-81)

NEW PROVIDENCE (see BAHAMAS) *Population:* 60,000. Language: English. 58 square miles in area, and the capital island of the Bahamas, New Providence lies about 200 miles east of Florida. The 17th century Bermudan settlers found piracy lucrative. The present population, 85% negro, produces enough fruit and vegetables for itself despite the poor soil. Nassau, the capital of the Bahamas, is on the island and caters for a large tourist trade.

ORKNEYS *Population:* 17,500. Language: English, with many Gaelic and Norse dialect words. County of Scotland. Of this group of 67 islands off the north coast of Scotland, 21 are inhabited, notably Mainland, Hoy, Sanday and Scapa. The islands were annexed to Scotland in 1472, when Christian I of Denmark pledged them as a dowry for his daughter at her marriage to James III of Scotland. The Danes continued to make claims on the islands until the mid-18th century. The islanders share a great sense of unity, calling themselves Orcadians. They are mostly crofters as the soil (though thin) is fertile, and the climate mild by virtue of the Gulf Stream. They export eggs, cattle and wool to the mainland. There is also a prosperous, sheltered fishing port at Stromness, and the well-protected naval harbor of Scapa Flow, where the German Fleet was scuppered by its own crews at the end of World War I.

PUERTO RICO *Population:* 2,800,000. Languages: Spanish, English. Autonomous part of the Commonwealth of USA since 1950. Puerto Rico is a densely populated island 70 miles east of Hispaniola. Just 3,435 square miles in area, it is the smallest and most easterly of the Greater Antilles. About one fifth of the population are of mainly negro descent, the remainder being of mulatto or Spanish stock. Many are engaged in the growing (American-aided) manufacturing and tourist industries, and the island enjoys the highest standard of living in the West Indies. But most Puerto Ricans are still employed as farm workers and work the large co-operative plantations, producing sugar, fruit, coffee and tobacco for export, and grow maize, beans and rice for home consumption. Emigration (to the US) is a traditional avenue to betterment. Since 1953, however, the birth rate, and emigration, have declined.

SAN SALVADOR (or WATLING ISLAND) (see BAHAMAS) *Population:* 1,500. Language: English. On the eastern side of the Bahamas about 350 miles south-east of the Florida coastline, San Salvador is thought to be the site of Columbus's first landing in America in 1492. There is now a US military installation on the island for tracking missiles launched from Cape Kennedy, 350 miles to the north-west. The island's soil is mostly infertile. The inhabitants, most of whom are negro, live by fishing.

ST CROIX *Population:* 15,000. Language: English. Unincorporated territory of USA. The largest of the Virgin Islands (80 square

miles), St Croix is about 70 miles south-east of Puerto Rico among the Leeward Islands. It was partly settled in the 16th century by Spanish, Dutch, English and French. The people, 90% negro and mulatto, still work mostly on sugar plantations, though tourism is important.
(pages 50-55)

SAINT HELENA *Population:* 5,000. Language: English. British colony with Gough Island and Tristan da Cunha. This south Atlantic island, 47 square miles, is 1,150 miles from the West African coast. It is famous as Napoleon's place of exile from 1815 to his death. The people are descended from European (mostly British) settlers and negro and Chinese slaves imported there in the 17th century by the British East India Company to grow flax. The islanders produce flax and rope for export. They grow potatoes and vegetables, and rear animals for their own consumption.

ST KILDA (see HEBRIDES) *Population:* nil. The lonely islands of this group, 60 miles west of Harris, are the furthest flung islands of Scotland: St Kilda, Soay, Boreray, Dun and high rocks called 'stacks'. All are surrounded by high cliffs with jagged shore lines indented with sea-caves. The flourishing population of the 17th century was virtually wiped out in 1724 by smallpox, brought to the island in the clothes of a St Kildan who died of the disease in Harris; and later contact with the mainland brought infant tetanus. Repeated emigrations were followed in 1930 by the evecuation to Argyll of the whole remaining population of fewer than 40 people. The island is now remarkable for its sea-birds.
(pages 130-135)

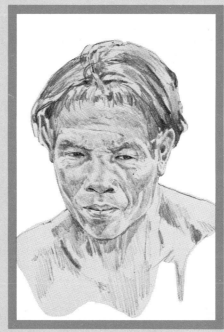

ST KITTS (see NEVIS) *Population:* 40,000. Language: English. Part of St Kitts-Nevis, British Associated State. St Kitts (or St Christopher), some 65 square miles in area, is in the Lesser Antilles Leeward Islands, two miles north-west of Nevis. The Caribs on the island were driven out within five years of it becoming a British colony in 1642 – the first in the Caribbean. The islanders are now predominately negro. The volcanic soils are fertile, but since the 18th century most of the land has been devoted to sugar cane and the islanders are unable to grow enough food for their needs.

ST LUCIA *Population:* 110,000. Languages: English, French *patois*. British Associated State. This island of the Lesser Antilles covers some 238 square miles, and lies 20 miles south of Martinique in the Windward Islands. Its indigenous Caribs were finally subjugated in the 18th century. It has on several occasions passed into French hands. The inhabitants are largely negro and mulatto. They grow bananas, sugar, coconuts and cocoa for export, and fruit and vegetables for their own markets.

ST PIERRE AND MIQUELON *Population:* 8,500. Language: French. French colony since 1763. These two small islands, just off the south coast of Newfoundland (10 miles from Burin), are the only remnants of France's possessions in Canada. They have always been important as depots for the French salt-cod fishermen. They have been a thorn in the side of successive Newfoundland governments; in 1904 a treaty that was part of the Entente Cordiale finally settled disputes over bait, lobster fishing and smuggling. Together the islands have an area of 93 square miles. St Pierre is the smaller and more important, 4 miles in diameter. Its main town is St Pierre, a port dominated by the fishing industry.
(pages 72-81)

ST VINCENT *Population:* 90,000. Language: English. British Associated State. St Vincent, which covers 150 square miles, is one of the Windward Islands in the Lesser Antilles, and lies 100 miles west of Barbados. A British force finally subdued the native Caribs in 1773. The population is 75% negro and 2.5% white and the rest are of mixed or East Indian extraction. Unusual in the Lesser Antilles. the island has an economic balance between large plantations (particularly of arrowroot) and peasant farming. About 200 pure Caribs survive today.

SAO TOMÉ AND PRINCIPÉ ISLANDS *Population:* 76,000. Languages: Portuguese, tribal languages. The islands, which cover 372 square miles, have been governed as a Portuguese province since 1522. The largest, São Tomé, lies about 120 miles west of the African continent. Principé Island is about 100 miles north-east of São Tomé. A slave trade to the coffee plantations caused a scandal as late as 1913. The islands are represented by a deputy in Lisbon.

SCILLY ISLES *Population:* 2,300. Language: English. County of England. The Scillies are 21 miles south-west of Land's End. The 140 islands and islets have an area of only 6.3 square miles, and only five are inhabited: St Mary's, Tresco, St Martin's, St Agnes and Bryher. The climate is the mildest of the British Isles, and by far the most important business on the islands is the cut flower trade: 582 acres on the islands are cultivated for flower crops. On the other hand, the islands are a treacherous hazard for shipping with many submerged rocks. Traditionally the population were wreckers. There is a saying that for every one Scillonian who dies a natural death, the sea takes nine.

SHETLANDS *Population:* 18,000. Language: English, with many Gaelic and Norse dialect words. County of Scotland. This group of about 100 islands and islets, which cover an area of 550 square miles, lies about 130 miles north of the Scottish mainland. The chief islands are Mainland, Yell and Unst. The islands' history of Norse invasion and occupation has left a strong imprint on language and culture. Crofting has lost its importance for the islanders' survival and the land is mainly given over to the famous Shetland sheep, whose wool has a world-wide market. The islanders knit by hand and weave tweed for export. Fishing is also important to their economy. The recent discovery of oil near Shetland augurs radical changes in the Shetlanders' lives.
(pages 92-99)

SKYE (see HEBRIDES) *Population:* 7,378. Languages: Gaelic, English. Part of Scotland. Skye is 643 square miles in area, the largest of the Inner Hebrides, separated from the west coast of Scotland by the narrow Sound of Sleat. Most of the land is moor and pasture, and Skye farmers are famed for their herds of West Highland cattle and black-faced sheep. The poor life of the crofters has been improved over the years by government grants, and Skye now attracts many tourists. Fishing and weaving are also important industries. While Portree is the main town and administration center, the seat of the principal clan, the MacLeods, is at Dunvegan.

SWAN ISLAND *Population:* 28. Language: English. US unincorporated territory. In the western Caribbean some 200 miles south of western Cuba and about 100 miles north of Honduras, this small island is just one mile square. The island has no native population and the inhabitants are chiefly employees of the United States Weather Service.

TRINIDAD AND TOBAGO *Population:* 1,200,000. Languages: English, French *patois*, French. Independent within the British Commonwealth. These islands lie in the south of the Caribbean, just north of Venezuela. Trinidad is 1,864 square miles and lies 18 miles south-west of its smaller neighbor Tobago, 116 square miles. The islands were settled first by Spaniards and negro slaves, received large numbers of French settlers in the 18th century, and were occupied by the British in 1797; the working class still use a French *patois*. Following the large influx of indentured east Indian workers throughout the 19th century, 36% of Trinidad people are Asians. There is also a 3% Chinese minority. A quarter of the people are employed in agriculture, mainly in family estates rather than as peasant farmers. Trinidad's industry is based largely on sea-drilled and imported oil from Venezuela, but the island also produces sugar, cocoa and rum, timber and fertilizers and is the world's largest source of asphalt. Trinidad still has a high rate of emigration unlike most of the Caribbean where emigration has declined since 1966.
(pages 28-33)

TRISTAN DA CUNHA *Population:* 260. Language: English. British colony since 1816. This small south Atlantic island, with an area of about 20 square miles, midway between South Africa and South America, was discovered by the Portuguese in 1506. It was first settled by a Scotsman, Corporal William Glass, and his Cape-colored wife, and the surname Glass is still one of only seven on the island. The islanders are of mixed origin. Their ancestors include a Dutchman, a negress, four mulatto women, American whalers, Genoese sailors, and a London cook. This variety is reflected in their looks. The islanders grow potatoes and some vegetables, and keep cattle, sheep, fowl and donkeys. After a volcanic eruption the entire population was evacuated to Britain, but returned to Tristan two years later in 1963.
(pages 112-119)

VIRGIN ISLANDS *Population:* 82,000. Language: English. This group of about 100 small islands in the Leeward Island group, only 14 of which are inhabited, is 40 miles east of Puerto Rico and extends for 60 miles. Uninhabited when discovered by Columbus, the islands are mostly dry and infertile. The principal British Virgin Islands (59 square miles) are Tortola, Virgin Gorda and Anegada, and the inhabitants, mostly negroes, raise cattle and fish. The principal American Virgin Islands (133 square miles) bought from Denmark in 1917 are St Thomas, St Croix, and St John. The sugar-plantations and tourist industry are subsidized by the US, and the population, which is mainly negro, does not produce enough food for its needs.

WINDWARD ISLANDS *Population:* 648,500. Language: English. Separate British Associated States. These islands, scattered between the Leeward Islands in the north and the outlying islands of Venezuela in the south, were to windward of the trading ships leaving the West Indies for Europe. They are Barbados, Grenada, the Grenadines, St Vincent and St Lucia. The islanders are, mainly negro and live by growing sugar for export, but tourism and the growth of the Venezuelan oil industry have brought more prosperity.

All population figures are approximate.